Reading Comprehension and Skills: Grade 2

Table of Contents

ISBN 978-1-60418-254-5

Ready-to-Use Ideas and Activities

This book was developed to help students master the basic skills necessary to become competent readers. The stronger their foundation in reading basics, the faster and easier children will be able to advance to more challenging texts.

Mastering the skills covered within the activity pages of this book is paramount for successful reading comprehension. The activities at the beginning of the book aim to build and reinforce vocabulary, the foundation of reading comprehension. These activities lead to practice with more advanced comprehension skills such as categorizing and using context to understand words. Then, at the end of the book, students begin to practice answering comprehension questions about progressively longer stories.

All children learn at their own rate; therefore, use your judgment to introduce concepts to children when developmentally appropriate.

Hands-on Learning

Hands-on learning reinforces the skills covered within the activity pages and improves students' potential for comprehension. One idea for a hands-on activity is to use the removable flash cards at the back of this book to play a game of bingo. To do this, make a copy of the bingo card on the next page for each student. Write the flash card words on the board and have students choose 24 of the words and write them in the empty spaces of their bingo cards in any order. When students have finished writing on their cards, gather the flash cards into a deck. Call out the words one at a time. Any student who has a word that you call out should make an *X* through the word on her card to cross it out. The student who crosses out five words in a row first (horizontally, vertically, or diagonally) wins the game by calling out, "Bingo!" To extend the game, you can continue playing until a student crosses out all of the words on his bingo card.

Comprehension Checks and Discussion

In addition to the activities in this book, you can support reading comprehension growth when you read stories in the classroom. After a story—or part of a story—is read, ask your students questions to ensure and enhance reading comprehension. The first type of question you might ask is a factual question. A factual question includes question words such as *who, what, when, where, how,* and *why.* For example, *How old is the character?, Where does the character live?, What time was it when…?,* or any other question that has a clear answer. You might also ask open-ended questions. These types of questions do not have a clear answer. They are based on opinions about the story, not on facts. For example, an open-ended question might be, *Why do you think the character acted as he did?, How do you think the character felt about her actions or the actions of others?, What do you think the character will do next?,* or *What other ways could this story have ended?*

 CD-104304 • © Carson-Dellosa

Vocabulary Bingo

		FREE		

Long a, e, and o

Look at the list of words below. Sort the words into three groups. Each group should have words with the same vowel sound.

day	phone	snake	feet
week	vote	neat	haste
speech	toe	fame	stone
meet	gale	treat	poke
case	make	snow	teeth
stale	seek	bone	grow

Long a Sound	**Long e Sound**	**Long o Sound**
_____	_____	_____
_____	_____	_____
_____	_____	_____
_____	_____	_____
_____	_____	_____
_____	_____	_____
_____	_____	_____

Think Ahead! List another word for each group.

_____   _____   _____

Name _____

Long i, u, and a

Look at the list of words below. Sort the words into three groups. Each group should have words with the same vowel sound.

blue	shade	ice	mine
cute	late	age	clue
game	strike	glue	knight
rice	fright	huge	skate
mule	tape	pride	rule
trade	bike	due	page

Long i Sound	**Long u Sound**	**Long a Sound**
_____	_____	_____
_____	_____	_____
_____	_____	_____
_____	_____	_____
_____	_____	_____
_____	_____	_____
_____	_____	_____

Think Ahead! List another word for each group.

_____   _____   _____

Short a, e, and o

Look at the list of words below. Sort the words into three groups. Each group should have words with the same vowel sound.

bad	hat	bed	hot
yell	block	plan	wet
black	floss	nest	flock
moth	clam	jog	stem
lamp	toss	stack	spell
pest	stock	nap	leg

Short a Sound	**Short e Sound**	**Short o Sound**
_____	_____	_____
_____	_____	_____
_____	_____	_____
_____	_____	_____
_____	_____	_____
_____	_____	_____
_____	_____	_____

Think Ahead! List another word for each group.

_____   _____   _____

CD-104304 • © Carson-Dellosa

Name _____

Short i, u, and a

Look at the list of words below. Sort the words into three groups. Each group should have words with the same vowel sound.

dust	drip	map	truck
quick	hand	rap	bun
trip	sack	club	win
quack	stuff	lip	pass
thumb	dish	cab	lunch
fist	fact	must	clip

Short i Sound	**Short u Sound**	**Short a Sound**
_____	_____	_____
_____	_____	_____
_____	_____	_____
_____	_____	_____
_____	_____	_____
_____	_____	_____
_____	_____	_____

Think Ahead! List another word for each group.

_____ _____ _____

Long or Short?

Look at the list of words below. Sort the words into two groups. Each group should have words with either short or long vowel sounds.

gate	cake	goat	wheat
pack	frog	wheel	sock
rug	time	bin	true
egg	own	gum	thumb
throat	man	cue	peg
mist	rate	nest	fine

Long Vowel Sounds   **Short Vowel Sounds**

_____ _____   _____ _____

_____ _____   _____ _____

_____ _____   _____ _____

_____ _____   _____ _____

_____ _____   _____ _____

_____ _____   _____ _____

Think Ahead!   List another word for each group.

_____   _____

Name _____

Long or Short?

Look at the list of words below. Sort the words into two groups. Each group should have words with either short or long vowel sounds.

mice	phone	top	blue
ear	mat	face	most
nose	light	fog	nap
pen	long	track	feet
duck	red	sit	cup
fuss	tube	paste	mine

Long Vowel Sounds   **Short Vowel Sounds**

_____ _____   _____ _____

_____ _____   _____ _____

_____ _____   _____ _____

_____ _____   _____ _____

_____ _____   _____ _____

_____ _____   _____ _____

Think Ahead!   **List another word for each group.**

_____   _____

ar, er, and ir

Look at the words in the list below. Sort the words into three groups. Each group should have words with *ar*, *er*, or *ir*.

govern	barn	herd	park
mark	first	squirm	danger
dart	serve	arm	circle
squirrel	swimmer	certain	dirt
bird	perhaps	firm	hard
jar	chirp	herself	cart

ar Sound   **er Sound**   **ir Sound**

_____ _____ _____

_____ _____ _____

_____ _____ _____

_____ _____ _____

_____ _____ _____

_____ _____ _____

_____ _____ _____

Think Ahead! Write a sentence that includes three of these words.

_____

CD-104304 • © Carson-Dellosa

Name _____

ur, ar, and _____

Look at the words in the list below. Sort the words with *ur* or *ar* into the first two groups. Look at the letters of the remaining words and label a third group. Write the words that belong in each group.

burr	artist	feather	return
power	part	shark	dancer
hunger	card	center	furry
turn	purpose	yard	farm
super	surprise	suffer	yarn
start	century	writer	slurp

ur Sound   **ar Sound**   _____

_____   _____   _____

_____   _____   _____

_____   _____   _____

_____   _____   _____

_____   _____   _____

_____   _____   _____

_____   _____   _____

Think Ahead! **Write a sentence that includes three of these words.**

_____

or, _____, and _____

Look at the words in the list below. Write the words with *or* in the first group. Look at the letters of the remaining words and label the second and third groups. Write the words that belong in each group.

darkness	storm	during	form
fork	burn	department	born
cartoon	purple	party	nurse
stork	turn	torn	sharp
curl	star	hurry	park
market	worn	doctor	fur

or Sound _____ _____

_____ _____ _____

_____ _____ _____

_____ _____ _____

_____ _____ _____

_____ _____ _____

_____ _____ _____

_____ _____ _____

Think Ahead! **Write a sentence that includes three of these words.**

_____

bl, cl, and fl

Look at the words in the list below. Sort the words into three groups. The words in each group should begin with the same blend.

flock	black	clear	blow
block	flood	blouse	flaw
blue	clerk	flat	closet
claim	flip	clover	flight
flash	cliff	blast	clue
blaze	clip	blueberry	floss

bl Sound   **cl Sound**   **fl Sound**

_____   _____   _____

_____   _____   _____

_____   _____   _____

_____   _____   _____

_____   _____   _____

_____   _____   _____

_____   _____   _____

Think Ahead!   Write a sentence that includes three of these words.

_____

gl, pl, and sl

Look at the words in the list below. Sort the words into three groups. The words in each group should begin with the same blend.

glove	pleasure	slip	glass
please	plop	slate	plus
pluck	glance	sleek	slide
sleep	place	glow	player
plentiful	gleam	slope	glue
glad	slow	gloom	slim

gl Sound   **pl Sound**   **sl Sound**

_____   _____   _____

_____   _____   _____

_____   _____   _____

_____   _____   _____

_____   _____   _____

_____   _____   _____

_____   _____   _____

Think Ahead!   **Write a sentence that includes three of these words.**

_____

Name _____

sh, sk, and st

Look at the words in the list below. Sort the words into three groups. The words in each group should begin with the same blend.

storm	share	skill	skip
shave	stink	sky	short
shovel	skate	shall	stale
skunk	shiver	skirt	stomach
stair	ski	steak	steam
skin	shirt	steep	shade

sh Sound　　　　　　**sk Sound**　　　　　　**st Sound**

_____   _____   _____

_____   _____   _____

_____   _____   _____

_____   _____   _____

_____   _____   _____

_____   _____   _____

_____   _____   _____

Think Ahead!　**Write a sentence that includes three of these words.**

_____

br, cr, and _____

Look at the words in the list below. Sort the words that begin with *br* or *cr* into the first two groups. Look at the letters of the remaining words and label a third group. Write the words that belong in each group.

dry	branch	crowd	drill
drip	brook	creep	craft
brown	crash	drove	crown
broom	crop	crow	brand
drift	brass	bread	dresser
crew	drink	dream	braid

br Sound   **cr Sound**   _____

_____   _____   _____

_____   _____   _____

_____   _____   _____

_____   _____   _____

_____   _____   _____

_____   _____   _____

_____   _____   _____

Think Ahead! Write a sentence that includes three of these words.

_____

Name _____

fr, gr, and _____

Look at the words in the list below. Sort the words that begin with *fr* or *gr* into the first two groups. Look at the letters of the remaining words and label a third group. Write the words that belong in each group.

proud	friendship	grant	frown
grandfather	freckles	problem	fry
grade	fright	preen	grape
produce	grasshopper	grin	fruit
grand	pretend	pride	promise
fresh	prowl	front	gruff

fr Sound   **gr Sound**   _____

_____   _____   _____

_____   _____   _____

_____   _____   _____

_____   _____   _____

_____   _____   _____

_____   _____   _____

_____   _____   _____

Think Ahead!   **Write a sentence that includes three of these words.**

_____

Name _____

str, thr, and _____

Look at the words in the list below. Sort the words that begin with *str* or *thr* into the first two groups. Look at the letters of the remaining words and label a third group. Write the words that belong in each group.

trouble	strike	through	trail
strange	trend	strength	throne
thread	throughout	treat	tryout
throw	straw	three	struggle
stream	trash	threw	street
trio	throat	triangle	strawberry

str Sound   **thr Sound**   _____

_____   _____   _____

_____   _____   _____

_____   _____   _____

_____   _____   _____

_____   _____   _____

_____   _____   _____

_____   _____   _____

Think Ahead!   **Write a sentence that includes three of these words.**

_____

Name _____

qu, _____, and _____

Look at the words in the list below. Write the words that begin with *qu* in the first group. Look at the letters of the remaining words and label the second and third groups. Write the words that belong in each group.

sweater	quail	squirm	question
quick	sweep	quite	swing
quiet	squash	sway	squeak
quarter	squirrel	swish	squid
sweet	squirt	swallow	squawk
swim	queen	square	quart

qu Sound   _____   _____

_____   _____   _____

_____   _____   _____

_____   _____   _____

_____   _____   _____

_____   _____   _____

_____   _____   _____

_____   _____   _____

Think Ahead!   **Write a sentence that includes three of these words.**

_____

ch, _____, and _____

Look at the words in the list below. Write the words that begin with *ch* in the first group. Look at the letters of the remaining words and label the second and third groups. Write the words that belong in each group.

thirty	charge	snug	thin
chirp	snake	chimney	thirsty
snack	snap	snail	chat
snowball	checkers	sniff	cheek
thick	cherry	thoughtful	thank
chance	third	thousand	snow

ch Sound _____ _____

_____ _____ _____

_____ _____ _____

_____ _____ _____

_____ _____ _____

_____ _____ _____

_____ _____ _____

_____ _____ _____

Think Ahead! **Write a sentence that includes three of these words.**

_____

ck, sh, and st

Look at the words in the list below. Sort the words into three groups. The words in each group should end with the same blend.

push	past	fresh	bash
first	pick	test	stock
cash	fish	flock	fast
sock	best	rock	flash
dish	must	clock	deck
mist	quick	dash	coast

ck Sound   **sh Sound**   **st Sound**

_____   _____   _____

_____   _____   _____

_____   _____   _____

_____   _____   _____

_____   _____   _____

_____   _____   _____

_____   _____   _____

_____   _____   _____

Think Ahead!   **Write a sentence that includes three of these words.**

_____

ch, ck, and _____

Look at the words in the list below. Sort the words that end with *ch* or *ck* into the first two groups. Look at the letters of the remaining words and label a third group. Write the words that belong in each group.

stack	pitch	cluck	branch
rich	struck	much	flash
squash	flock	fresh	quack
which	wish	such	dash
click	trash	block	crash
mash	back	itch	batch

ch Sound   **ck Sound**   _____

_____   _____   _____

_____   _____   _____

_____   _____   _____

_____   _____   _____

_____   _____   _____

_____   _____   _____

_____   _____   _____

Think Ahead! **Write a sentence that includes three of these words.**

_____

Name _____

Ending Clusters

nt, _____, and _____

Look at the words in the list below. Write the words that end with *nt* in the first group. Look at the letters of the remaining words and label the second and third groups. Write the words that belong in each group.

hunt	brand	rent	think
almond	grant	island	dent
spend	pink	giant	ink
drank	paint	wink	talent
mount	stink	hound	yank
command	around	thank	found

nt Sound _____ _____

_____ _____ _____

_____ _____ _____

_____ _____ _____

_____ _____ _____

_____ _____ _____

_____ _____ _____

_____ _____ _____

Think Ahead! **Write a sentence that includes three of these words.**

_____

CD-104304 • © Carson-Dellosa

Name _____

Read the story below. Decide which word in the box below means almost the same thing as each underlined word or phrase in the story. Write your answers below the story.

contests	baking	go	enjoy
unhappy	playground	chilly	

Summer

       1   **2**   **3**   **4**

I <u>like</u> summer. My friends and I play <u>games</u> in the <u>park</u>. The sun is <u>hot</u>, but the

      5   **6**   **7**

pool is <u>cool</u>. We are <u>sad</u> when it is time to <u>leave</u>.

1. _____   5. _____

2. _____   6. _____

3. _____   7. _____

4. _____

Draw a picture to go with the story.

Read the story below. Decide which word in the box below means almost the same thing as each underlined word or phrase in the story. Write your answers below the story.

several	rest	closest
street	yellow	younger
tunes	pestering	giant

My Best Friend

1
My best friend's name is Sally. She has blond hair and green eyes. Sally lives
3   4   5   6
down the road from me in a big house. We like to sit in her room and play songs.
7   8   9
Sally has some little brothers who are always bothering us.

1. _____

2. _____

3. _____

4. _____

5. _____

6. _____

7. _____

8. _____

9. _____

Draw a picture to go with the story.

Read the story below. Decide which word in the box below means almost the same thing as each underlined word or phrase in the story. Write your answers below the story.

slice	cup	mother	super
hotcakes	complete	father	beginning

Eating Breakfast

Every morning, my <u>mom</u>[1] wakes me up for breakfast. I have a <u>glass</u>[2] of juice and a <u>piece</u>[3] of toast. Sometimes my <u>dad</u>[4] makes <u>pancakes</u>[5] with bananas. A <u>balanced</u>[6] breakfast gets the day off to a <u>great</u>[7] <u>start</u>[8]!

I. _____

2. _____

3. _____

4. _____

5. _____

6. _____

7. _____

8. _____

Draw a picture to go with the story.

Name _____

Read the story below. Decide which word in the box below means almost the same thing as each underlined word or phrase in the story. Write your answers below the story.

```
takes        each        bright       pals
neighbor     pretty      stormy       travel
```

Going to School

My friends and I go to school in different ways. Trey's mother drives him in her black truck. Jan rides the bus with a girl next door. Tara and Miguel walk to school if the weather is nice. I ride my bicycle every day whether it is rainy or sunny!

1. _____   5. _____

2. _____   6. _____

3. _____   7. _____

4. _____   8. _____

Draw a picture to go with the story.

Name _____

Read the story below. Decide which word in the box below means almost the same thing as each underlined word or phrase in the story. Write your answers below the story.

> air   lumber   bound   thin
> rope   high   pasted   youth

Flying a Kite

When my father was a boy[1], he flew kites. He and his brother took a ball of string[2] and some narrow[3] wood. They cut the wood[4] into a square. Then, they glued[5] colorful paper on it. Finally, they tied[6] a tail on the kite. The kite would fly up[7] in the sky[8]!

1. _____

2. _____

3. _____

4. _____

5. _____

6. _____

7. _____

8. _____

Draw a picture to go with the story.

Name _____

Read the story below. Decide which word in the box below means almost the same thing as each underlined word or phrase in the story. Write your answers below the story.

pick	large	spotless	box	hop
small	vacation	crying	just	states

Our New Kittens

Over spring break¹, our cat had kittens. They were tiny², and they made squeaking³ sounds instead of meows. She licked their faces to keep them clean⁴. They stayed in a basket⁵ until they were big⁶ enough to jump⁷ out. Mom says⁸ that we can keep only⁹ one. It is hard to decide¹⁰ which one!

1. _____

2. _____

3. _____

4. _____

5. _____

6. _____

7. _____

8. _____

9. _____

10. _____

Draw a picture to go with the story.

Read the story below. Decide which word in the box below means almost the same thing as each underlined word or phrase in the story. Write your answers below the story.

> eat   grow   bit   earth   till
> visit   shoveling   splash   owns   stony

Aunt Jill's Farm

             1   2   3

Aunt Jill has a piece of land in the country. When we go see her, we help her

4   5   6   7

farm the soil. The ground can be rocky, so digging is hard. We plant the seeds

        8   9   10

and spray them with water. After they get bigger, we can dine on them!

1. _____   6. _____

2. _____   7. _____

3. _____   8. _____

4. _____   9. _____

5. _____   10. _____

Draw a picture to go with the story.

Name _____

Read the story below. Decide which word in the box below means almost the same thing as each underlined word or phrase in the story. Write your answers below the story.

> class   buy   company   work   papers
> read   produce   house   articles   notes

Dad's Computer

Dad showed me how to <u>use</u>[1] the computer at his <u>business</u>[2]. I can type <u>letters</u>[3] to my friends. I can <u>look at</u>[4] funny <u>stories</u>[5] on the Internet. I can <u>prepare</u>[6] <u>reports</u>[7] for school too. I wish we could <u>get</u>[9] a computer for our <u>home</u>[10]!

(Note: underlined words numbered 1–10: use(1) business(2) letters(3) look at(4) stories(5) prepare(6) reports(7) school(8) get(9) home(10))

1. _____   6. _____

2. _____   7. _____

3. _____   8. _____

4. _____   9. _____

5. _____   10. _____

Draw a picture to go with the story.

Name _____

Read the story below. Decide which word in the box below means almost the same thing as each underlined word or phrase in the story. Write your answers below the story.

nightfall	high	trail	hear
bring	notice	pounding	night
happy	woods	run	hound

Jogging with Mom

Mom and I like to jog every evening. We sometimes take our dog, Rudy. We
turn down a path and jog through the forest. We see the tall trees and listen to our
feet hitting the ground. Being outside at sundown makes me feel joyful.

1. _____   7. _____

2. _____   8. _____

3. _____   9. _____

4. _____   10. _____

5. _____   11. _____

6. _____   12. _____

Draw a picture to go with the story.

Name _____

Read the story below. Rewrite the story by replacing each underlined word with a word from the list that means the opposite.

windy	light	his	he	your
dark	boy	wet	ocean	

My Book

I am writing <u>my</u> book. It is about a <u>girl</u> named Taylor. <u>She</u> has <u>light</u> hair and <u>dark</u> eyes. <u>Her</u> family lives by the <u>desert</u>. It is very <u>dry</u> there and the air is <u>still</u>.

_____

_____

_____

_____

_____

My Book

Name _____

Read the story below. Rewrite the story by replacing each underlined word with a word from the list that means the opposite.

autumn	cold	plant	less
dies	inside	slowly	old

Seasons

I like spring more than other seasons. The leaves are young. The grass grows quickly. We pick flowers for Mom. We go outside and watch the warm rain.

_____

_____

_____

_____

_____

Name _____

Read the story below. Rewrite the story by replacing each underlined word with a word from the list that means the opposite.

frown	short	slowly	lost	new
dislike	never	yell	sad	

Book Buddies

My friends and I <u>always</u> <u>talk</u> about what we are reading. I am reading a <u>long</u> book about the jungle. It is going <u>quickly</u>. Joe is reading a <u>funny</u> book. We <u>smile</u> a lot when he talks about it. Rita <u>found</u> an <u>old</u> book at her grandparents' house. We all <u>like</u> the books she reads.

_____

_____

_____

_____

_____

_____

Read the story below. Rewrite the story by replacing each underlined word with a word from the list that means the opposite.

her	poorly	she	sold	to
sister	woman	dislike	old	

Pat's Car

My <u>brother</u> Pat has a car. <u>He</u> <u>bought</u> it <u>from</u> a <u>man</u> named Chris. Pat's car is <u>new</u>. The car runs <u>smoothly</u>. I <u>like</u> riding in <u>his</u> car.

_____

_____

_____

_____

Name _____

Read the story below. Rewrite the story by replacing each underlined word with a word from the list that means the opposite.

sunset	back	few	sit
country	large	summer	evening

Lynn's House

My friend Lynn lives in the <u>city</u>. Lynn has a <u>tiny</u> house with <u>lots of</u> neighbors. My cat and I go see Lynn every <u>winter</u>. In the <u>morning</u>, we like to <u>stand</u> out <u>front</u>. We like to look at the <u>sunrise</u>.

_____

_____

_____

_____

_____

Read the story below. Rewrite the story by replacing each underlined word with a word from the list that means the opposite.

left	lost	sad	nothing
dark	last	quiet	huge

A Special Puppy

Last week, I <u>found</u> a <u>little</u> puppy. He has <u>bright</u> eyes and a <u>loud</u> bark. He is brown with a white dot on his <u>right</u> leg. We <u>first</u> saw him in our backyard. He seemed to be looking for <u>something</u>. The puppy looked <u>happy</u>.

_____

_____

_____

_____

_____

Name _____

Read the story below. Rewrite the story by replacing each underlined word with a word from the list that means the opposite.

few	ran	bottom	right-side-out
under	nobody	slept	late

Opposite Day

Today was opposite day at school. I <u>woke</u> <u>early</u> and <u>walked</u> to class. <u>Everyone</u> wore their pants <u>inside-out</u>. <u>Many</u> people wore their socks <u>over</u> their pants. My teacher even put shoes on the <u>top</u> of her desk!

_____

_____

_____

_____

_____

Name _____

Read the story below. Rewrite the story by replacing each underlined word or phrase with a word or phrase from the list that means the opposite.

stop	scatter	take down	sometimes
leave	packs	up	day
ahead of	breakfast	east	end

Camping

My family <u>often</u> goes camping. We leave after <u>dinner</u> and drive all <u>night</u>. We drive <u>west</u> and watch the sun come <u>down</u> <u>behind</u> us. We <u>arrive</u> where we camp in the afternoon. We <u>put up</u> our tent. We <u>gather</u> wood and <u>start</u> a fire. My family <u>unpacks</u> the rest of our things to <u>begin</u> our trip.

_____

_____

_____

_____

_____

_____

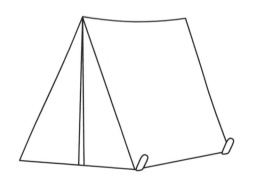

Name _____

Read the story below. Rewrite the story by replacing each underlined word with a word from the list that means the opposite.

strong	rotten	bad	awake
forgot	lost	result	poorly

Janelle's Day

Janelle had a <u>wonderful</u> day. She played a game with a friend and <u>won</u>. She ate <u>fresh</u> fruit. She <u>remembered</u> to take out the trash. She even discovered that a skunk was the <u>cause</u> of a <u>weak</u> smell in her yard! Now Janelle felt <u>sleepy</u>. She will sleep <u>well</u> tonight.

_____

_____

_____

_____

_____

_____

Name _____

1. Read the story.

Picnic

My family decided to go on a picnic. I started baking cookies right away. Mom packed bread and meat for sandwiches. Then, Dad put everything in the car. We picked up Grandma.

2. Read the sentences below. Write them in order as they happened in the story.

Mom packed meat and bread.
I baked cookies.
We picked up Grandma.
We decided to go on a picnic.
Dad packed the car.

1. _____

2. _____

3. _____

4. _____

5. _____

3. Draw a line under the best ending for this story.

We all had a good time.
We went to the zoo.
Grandma brought cookies.

I. Read the story.

Writing a Story

My sister and I got out paper and pencils to write a story. First, we thought of a character. Then, we talked about what the character looked like. Next, we thought of something our character could do. Finally, we thought of a good ending.

2. Read the sentences below. Write them in order as they happened in the story.

We thought of a good ending.

We thought of a character.

We decided what our character would do.

We got out paper and pencils.

We talked about the character's looks.

I. _____

2. _____

3. _____

4. _____

5. _____

3. Draw a line under the best ending for this story.

Our character had yellow hair.

We read our story to our dad.

We wrote our story with a pencil.

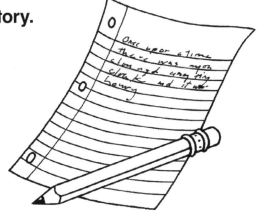

Name _____

1. Read the story.

Getting Ready for School

My mom wakes me up for school. I get out of bed and brush my teeth. I put on my shirt and pants. I eat toast and fruit for breakfast. My stepdad makes sure I put my homework in my bag.

2. Read the sentences below. Write them in order as they happened in the story.

I eat toast and fruit.
I put on my shirt.
I put my homework in my bag.
My mom wakes me up.
I brush my teeth.

1. _____

2. _____

3. _____

4. _____

5. _____

3. Draw a line under the best ending for this story.

Then, I catch the bus.
Mom cooks dinner.
Then, I go to sleep.

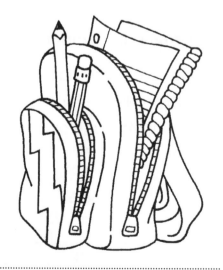

Name _____

1. Read the story.

Birthday Party

Emily turned eight years old last weekend. Today, she had a birthday party. Everyone came at noon. They sang "Happy Birthday" to Emily and ate cake. Then, they played games outside. Some people stayed to sing songs.

2. Read the sentences below. Write them in order as they happened in the story.

Emily turned eight.
They played outside.
They sang and ate cake.
They came to Emily's party.
They sang songs.

1. _____

2. _____

3. _____

4. _____

5. _____

3. Draw a line under the best ending for this story.

Emily's brother went to the store.
The teacher asked Emily to stay late.
Emily thanked her friends for coming.

1. Read the story.

A Gift

My teacher is Miss Wong. Our class wanted to give her a gift. Wayne thought a fish in an aquarium would be nice. April wanted to buy a pen. Mario said that we should make her a sign. We liked that idea best. We wrote, "We love you, Miss Wong!"

2. Read the sentences below. Write them in order as they happened in the story.

Wayne wanted to buy a fish.
Mario said to make her a sign.
April wanted to buy a pen.
We wanted to give Miss Wong a gift.
We wrote, "We love you, Miss Wong!"

1. _____

2. _____

3. _____

4. _____

5. _____

3. Draw a line under the best ending for this story.

Miss Wong was not at school today.
We gave her a pet hamster.
Miss Wong was proud of the sign.

Name _____

1. Read the story.

Fruit Salad

Dad taught me how to make fruit salad. We bought the fruit at the store. We washed it in the sink. Dad cut up the apples. Next, he cut up the oranges. Then, he cut up the bananas. We put them in a bowl with grapes and cherries.

2. Read the sentences below. Write them in order as they happened in the story.

We put the fruit in a bowl.

Dad cut up the oranges.

We washed the fruit.

We bought the fruit.

Dad cut up the apples.

1. _____

2. _____

3. _____

4. _____

5. _____

3. Draw a line under the best ending for this story.

Dad cut up some more apples.

The salad tasted great!

We washed the bananas.

47

Name _____

I. Read the story.

Painting My Bedroom

Mom said that I could paint my bedroom. She said that she would help me. We borrowed brushes and bought cans of paint. We changed into old clothes. We rubbed the walls with sandpaper. This made them smooth. We painted the walls green and the trim blue.

2. Read the sentences below. Write them in order as they happened in the story.

We borrowed brushes.
We rubbed the walls.
We painted the walls and trim.
We changed into old clothes.
Mom said that I could paint my room.

I. _____

2. _____

3. _____

4. _____

5. _____

3. Draw a line under the best ending for this story.

My new room looks great.
I put on my old jeans.
My sister likes the color orange.

Name _____

1. Read the story.

Planting a Garden

I help Grandpa plant his summer garden. First, we go to the store to buy seeds. We rake the soil. We dig holes and plant the seeds. Then, we cover the seeds with dirt. We water the seeds so they will grow.

2. Read the sentences below. Write them in order as they happened in the story.

We water the seeds.

We rake the soil.

We buy the seeds.

We cover the seeds with dirt.

We plant the seeds.

1. _____

2. _____

3. _____

4. _____

5. _____

3. Draw a line under the best ending for this story.

Grandpa buys a lot of seeds.

Soon, we will have vegetables to eat!

We buy a new rake.

1. Read the story.

Putting on a Play

Tammy was in her class play. She was picked to play the queen. She practiced her lines so that she could remember them. The night of the play arrived. She got dressed like a queen. Her dad, stepmom, and brother came to watch.

2. Read the sentences below. Write them in order as they happened in the story.

She got dressed.

She practiced her lines.

Tammy was chosen to play the queen.

The night of the play arrived.

Her family came.

1. _____

2. _____

3. _____

4. _____

5. _____

3. Draw a line under the best ending for this story.

Tammy's mother made her a new dress.

Her friend played the king.

The crowd clapped for the actors.

Name _____

1. Read the story.

A New School

My family moved to a new town. I went to a new school. A nice teacher met me at the door. She helped me find my classroom. At lunch, I made a new friend named Ana.

2. Read the sentences below. Write them in order as they happened in the story.

She helped me find my classroom.

I went to a new school.

My family moved.

I made a new friend.

I met a nice teacher.

1. _____

2. _____

3. _____

4. _____

5. _____

3. Draw a line under the best ending for this story.

Now, Ana and I are best friends.

My brother is named Dave.

I wore a new skirt on the first day.

Name _____

Read the story. Then, answer the questions.

Heath is a fast runner. He always wins his class race. A new girl came to Heath's class. Her name was Marisa. She was the fastest runner at her old school. Heath wondered if she could run as fast as him. They had a race after school. Heath and Marisa tied! Now they are best friends.

1. What is a good title for this story?
   a. Marisa's Old School
   b. New Friends
   c. First Place

2. What did Heath wonder?

   _____

3. What did Heath and Marisa do?

   a. _____

   b. _____

4. What do Heath and Marisa have in common?

   _____

5. How do you think Heath felt when Marisa came to his class?

   _____

   _____

Name _____

Read the story. Then, answer the questions.

Ethan liked to stop by Grandma's house after school. She would fix him a snack. One day, Grandma fell and broke her arm. The doctor said that she needed to rest. Grandma came to stay with Ethan and his mom until she felt better. Now, Ethan fixes Grandma a snack every afternoon.

1. What is a good title for this story?
   a. Helping Grandma
   b. Ethan's Snack
   c. Grandma's Doctor

2. What did Ethan like to do?

   _____

3. What happened to Grandma?

   _____

   _____

4. Where did Grandma stay while she was hurt?

   _____

   _____

5. Name something else Ethan could do to help Grandma.

   _____

Name _____

Read the story. Then, answer the questions.

Kassie wanted a new puppy. Her mom said that she could get a small one. Kassie picked out a tiny gray puppy named Ruff. Ruff liked to eat. He was always hungry. He got bigger and bigger, until he was almost as tall as Kassie. Kassie said, "I thought we got a small dog!" Mom smiled and said, "You will have to grow bigger to take care of him!"

1. What is a good title for this story?
   a. Kassie's Tiny Puppy
   b. Ruff Liked to Eat
   c. A Big Surprise

2. What kind of dog did Mom want Kassie to get?

   _____

3. What happened to Ruff?

   _____

   _____

4. What did Mom tell Kassie she would need to do at the end of the story?

   _____

   _____

5. What are two ways you can take care of a dog?

   _____

   _____

Name _____

Read the story. Then, answer the questions.

Vanessa's brother Luke is in the army. He visits countries that are far away. He helps people who need food or doctors. One day, Luke surprised Vanessa. She did not know he was home for a break. He came to Vanessa's school wearing his uniform. She was happy to see him standing in the doorway of the lunchroom. Everyone said that she was a lucky girl.

1. What is a good title for this story?
    a. Army Life
    b. Vanessa's Special Treat
    c. Luke's Uniform

2. What are two things that Luke does in the army?

    a. _____

    b. _____

3. Why was Vanessa surprised?

    _____

4. What word means the same as *uniform*?
    a. shoes
    b. army
    c. outfit

5. Why did everyone say that Vanessa was a lucky girl?

    _____

    _____

Name _____

Read the story. Then, answer the questions.

It was a sunny day. Sarah and her friends played outside at recess. When it was time to go inside, they heard a clap of thunder. All afternoon, they heard the rain outside. Sarah wondered if she would have to catch the bus in the rain. Her umbrella was at home. After school, Sarah and her friends lined up to leave. It was still raining. Sarah put her coat over her head and ran for the bus. She found a way to stay dry after all!

1. What is a good title for this story?
   a. Umbrellas
   b. Catching the Bus
   c. Sarah's Bright Idea

2. What two things did Sarah and her friends hear?

   a. _____

   b. _____

3. What did Sarah wonder?

   _____

   _____

4. What did Sarah do to keep dry?

   _____

5. What is another way to keep dry without an umbrella?

   _____

Name _____

Read the story. Then, answer the questions.

Jared's mother teaches at his school. Every morning, Jared and his mom ride to school together. One morning, his mom had a cold and could not go to school. Jared called his friend Juan and asked for a ride. Juan lived down the street from Jared. Juan's uncle usually took Juan to school. Juan's uncle was sick too! Jared had an idea. He asked his mom to help him look up the school bus schedule on the World Wide Web. Jared told Juan to meet him at the bus stop in 5 minutes. They rode to school together on the bus.

1. What is a good title for this story?
    a. Jared's Good Idea
    b. Get Well, Jared
    c. Jared and Juan Ride the Train

2. Which two people are sick in the story?

    a. _____

    b. _____

3. What was Jared's idea?

    _____

4. Where did Jared find the bus schedule?

    _____

5. What might have happened if Jared and Juan got to the bus stop in 10 minutes instead of 5 minutes?

    _____

    _____

Name _____

Read the story. Then, answer the questions.

Last week, my class took a trip to the zoo. We went to the snake house. Some people were scared, but not me! I knew we were safe. The snakes were behind the glass. We fed peanuts to the baby goats and watched the monkeys swing from branch to branch. Sometimes, my father calls me a monkey, and now I know why! I wanted to ask my gymnastics coach to teach me some tricks I saw the monkeys do.

1. What is a good title for this story?
   a. The Snake House
   b. Monkey See, Monkey Do
   c. Baby Goats

2. What three animals did the children see at the zoo?

   a. _____

   b. _____

   c. _____

3. Why does the writer know they are safe from the snakes?

   _____

4. What does the writer want to do after seeing the monkeys?

   _____

   _____

5. Why do you think the writer's father calls him a monkey?

   _____

Name _____

Read the story. Then, answer the questions.

    I have a funny cat named Sam. He imagines that he is a dog! He likes to run after balls that jingle. He brings them back when I throw them. He chases his tail. He even growls at the mailman! Sam's best friend is my little brother, Robert. He follows Robert around the house and sleeps on his bed. Robert wants to teach Sam to walk on a leash. We are sure he can learn!

1. What is a good title for this story?
    a. Cat or Dog?
    b. Robert's Best Friend
    c. The Mailman

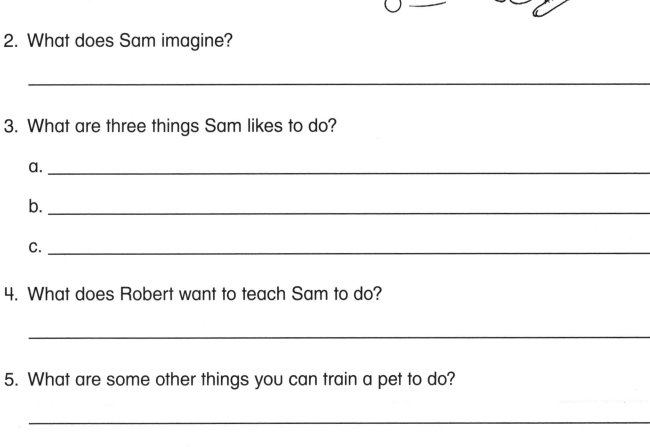

2. What does Sam imagine?

   _____

3. What are three things Sam likes to do?

    a. _____

    b. _____

    c. _____

4. What does Robert want to teach Sam to do?

   _____

5. What are some other things you can train a pet to do?

   _____

   _____

Name _____

Read the story. Then, answer the questions.

Our school has a new club. It meets every Tuesday after school. It is not a sports club. It is not a science club. It is a community club! The club members help our town by cleaning up litter. The members read to older people and visit sick neighbors. The mayor came to the first meeting. She is happy the club is helping others. I want to join the club so that I can be helpful.

1. What is a good title for this story?
    a. Cleaning Up Litter
    b. The Mayor's Letter
    c. The Community Club

2. What is another word for *community*?
    a. neighborhood
    b. sports
    c. science

3. What are three things the club members do?

    a. _____

    b. _____

    c. _____

4. Why does the writer want to join the club?

    _____

5. What are some other things you can do to help your community?

    _____

    _____

Name _____

Read the story. Then, answer the questions.

My grandpa was a firefighter for a long time. He helped save people from burning houses. Sometimes, he carried people down a ladder. Now, he has a new job. He does not go into burning buildings anymore. Grandpa visits schools to share knowledge about fire safety. He shows them the burn marks on his old jacket. He tells everyone how to stay safe. My grandpa is a hero.

1. What is a good title for this story?
   a. Fire Safety
   b. Grandpa's New Job
   c. An Old Jacket

2. What did Grandpa do at his old job?

   _____

3. Why does Grandpa visit schools?

   _____

4. What are two things Grandpa does at the schools he visits?

   a. _____

   b. _____

5. Why do you think the writer says Grandpa is a hero?

   _____

Name _____

Read the story. Then, answer the questions.

Brian's little sister Kayce started school this year. They go to the same school. Brian introduced Kayce to his friends at school. His friends thought she was a pleasure to be around. Some of them had little sisters in kindergarten too. They introduced Kayce to their sisters. Kayce was happy to have new friends. She was also happy to have a brother like Brian. She hoped that she could introduce someone to a new friend!

1. What is a good title for this story?
   a. Kayce's Little Friend
   b. New Introductions
   c. Bothering Brian

2. What does Brian do to help Kayce?

   _____

   _____

3. How did Brian's friends feel about Kayce?

   _____

4. What did Brian and some of his friends have in common?

   _____

5. Why do you think Kayce would like to introduce someone to a new friend?

   _____

   _____

Name _____

Read the story. Then, answer the questions.

Teeth

Teeth are important for chewing food, so you need to take care of your teeth. When you are a child, you have baby teeth. These fall out and are replaced by adult teeth. You can expect to have a full set of 32 teeth one day. Brush your teeth twice a day, in the morning and at bedtime. Also, floss to remove the bits of food that get stuck between your teeth. That way, you will have a healthy smile!

1. What is the main idea of this story?
    a. You can have a healthy smile.
    b. It is important to take care of your teeth.
    c. Adults have more teeth than children.

2. Why should you take care of your teeth?

    _____

3. What happens to baby teeth?

    _____

4. How many teeth do adults have?

    _____

5. How often should you brush your teeth?
    a. only at lunchtime
    b. once a week
    c. twice a day

6. How does flossing help keep your teeth healthy?

    _____

    _____

Read the story. Then, answer the questions.

Sleep

   Are you ever sleepy in class? Children need about 10 hours of sleep each night. It is important to be rested for school every morning. If you are tired, you will have trouble paying attention to your teacher. If you have a hard time falling asleep, try reading a book instead of watching TV before bedtime. Go to bed at the same time every night. Ask your family to play soft music to help you get sleepy. Soon, you will be dreaming!

1. What is the main idea of this story?
   a. Getting enough sleep is important for good health.
   b. Reading a book can help you sleep.
   c. You should dream every night.

2. How much sleep do children need?

   _____

3. What might happen at school if you are tired?

   _____

   _____

4. What can you do instead of watching TV at bedtime?

   _____

5. When should you go to bed?
   a. 10 P.M.
   b. only when you feel sleepy
   c. at the same time every night

6. What can your family do to help you get sleepy?

   _____

Name _____

Read the story. Then, answer the questions.

Exercise

Exercising is a great way to take care of your body. It is something the whole family can do together. You should try to exercise for a little while each day. Some fun things to do are running, jumping rope, or walking a dog. You might enjoy playing sports with your friends. Kickball and basketball are good team sports to try. If you start exercising now, you will be used to it when you get older!

1. What is the main idea of this story?
    a. Everyone should exercise each day.
    b. You might like to play basketball.
    c. You should exercise to take care of your body.

2. What is something your whole family can do?

    _____

3. How often should you exercise?

    _____

4. What are some fun ways to exercise?

    _____

5. What is a team sport?

    _____

    _____

6. If you start exercising now, what will happen when you get older?

    _____

    _____

Read the story. Then, answer the questions.

Talking It Out

Sometimes, our friends can make us angry or hurt our feelings. Instead of fighting with someone who upsets you, try to talk it out. Ask a teacher or another friend to help you talk to each other. Tell them why you are upset. Your friend may be upset about something you said or did too. Listen to their words calmly. After all, you want them to listen to you too! When both of you are done talking, shake hands and forgive each other.

1. What is the main idea of this story?
   a. Talking out a problem is better than fighting.
   b. Ask a teacher to help.
   c. Your friend may be upset too.

2. What should you do if someone upsets you?

   _____

3. Who can you ask for help?

   _____

4. Why should you listen to your friend's words calmly?

   _____

5. What should you do after you are both done talking?

   _____

   _____

6. What might happen if you get into a fight with someone who made you angry?

   _____

   _____

Name _____

Read the story. Then, answer the questions.

Wash Your Hands

You have most likely heard your family and teachers tell you to wash your hands. Be sure to use warm water and soap. Rub your hands together for as long as it takes to sing the A-B-Cs. Then, sing the song again while you rinse them. Soap can help kill the germs, or tiny bugs, that make you sick. If you do not wash your hands, you can pass along an illness to a friend. You could also spread the germs to your eyes or mouth if you touch them before washing your hands. Remember to wash your hands!

1. What is the main idea of this story?
    a. Bugs can make you sick.
    b. Rub your hands together.
    c. You should wash your hands with warm water and soap.

2. How long should you rub your hands together?

   _____

3. What does soap do?

   _____

4. What does the word *germs* mean?
    a. kinds of soap
    b. tiny bugs that can make you sick
    c. ways to wash your hands

5. What could happen if you don't wash your hands?

   _____

6. Why should you not touch your face before washing your hands?

   _____

Read the story. Then, answer the questions.

Colds

Catching a cold is not fun. You may have red eyes, a sore throat, and a runny nose. You may want to lie in bed all afternoon and sleep. Your voice might sound funny. There are a few things you can do to get better a little faster. First, get plenty of sleep. Your body needs rest to heal itself. Also, drink lots of water or juice. Warm soup is good for you when you are sick too. Most of all, respect your doctor's orders!

1. What is the main idea of this story?
   a. You should lie in bed all afternoon.
   b. Take care of your body when you have a cold.
   c. Everyone gets sick every now and then.

2. What are some signs of a cold?

   _____

   _____

3. What might happen to your voice when you have a cold?

   _____

4. Why should you get plenty of sleep when you are sick?

   _____

5. What should you eat and drink?

   _____

6. Why should you respect your doctor's orders?

   _____

   _____

Read the story. Then, answer the questions.

Food for Thought

What do you like to eat? You may want a candy bar and a soda after school. These foods have a lot of sugar in them. The sugar perks you up, but it wears off quickly. You will feel tired later, when it is time to do your homework. A better snack is a glass of milk and a sandwich. You might have some carrots or grapes too. Your body will thank you for the good snack.

1. What is the main idea of this story?
   a. Think about what you eat.
   b. Sugar wears off quickly.
   c. Your body will thank you.

2. What do candy bars and soda have in them?

   _____

3. What does sugar do to your body?

   _____

4. What is a good snack after school?

   _____

5. Which of these foods is a vegetable?
   a. grape
   b. milk
   c. carrot

6. Why might someone choose a candy bar and a soda after school?

   _____

   _____

Read the story. Then, answer the questions.

Healthy Heart and Lungs

Your heart and lungs are important parts of the body. The heart moves blood through the body. Without lungs, you could not breathe. You must exercise to keep your heart and lungs healthy. Your heart starts beating faster when you run fast or jump rope. You may breathe harder too. It is good to make your heart and lungs work harder sometimes. This makes them stronger, and you will also feel healthier. Keeping yourself healthy can be a lifelong practice so that you can have a long life.

1. What is the main idea of this story?
    a. Your heart works harder when you run.
    b. Without lungs, you could not breathe.
    c. Exercising keeps your heart and lungs healthy.

2. What does the heart do in the body?

   _____

3. What do lungs help you do?

   _____

4. What happens to your heart when you run fast?
    a. It starts beating faster.
    b. It stops and starts.
    c. It makes you breathe harder.

5. What happens to your lungs when you jump rope?

   _____

6. Why is it good to make your heart work hard sometimes?

   _____

Read the story. Then, answer the questions.

The Five Senses

Most people have five senses: sight, sound, smell, taste, and touch. You see with your eyes. You hear with your ears. You smell with your nose. You taste with your tongue, and you touch with your hands. If you have a cold, your sense of smell might not work right. This makes things taste funny too. You want to protect your senses. Keep sharp objects away from your eyes. Turn down the music before it hurts your ears. Never touch a hot stove with your bare hands.

1. What is the main idea of this story?
   a. The five senses help you understand the world.
   b. Never listen to loud music.
   c. You smell with your nose and see with your eyes.

2. What are the five senses?

   _____

   _____

3. What does your tongue help you do?

   _____

4. What might happen to your senses when you have a cold?

   _____

   _____

5. How can you keep your sense of sight safe?

   _____

6. Why should you not touch a hot stove?

   _____

Read the story. Then, answer the questions.

Going to the Doctor

Your family takes you to the doctor when you are sick. They should also take you when you are well. You should visit the doctor every year to make sure your body is healthy. The doctor will measure how tall you have grown and how much you weigh. She will look at your eyes, ears, and mouth. She will listen to your heart and lungs. Do not be afraid to go to the doctor. She wants you to stay well so that you do not have to see her more often.

1. What is the main idea of this story?
   a. She will see how tall you have grown.
   b. Going to the doctor can keep you healthy.
   c. The doctor will look at your eyes.

2. When does your family take you to the doctor?

   _____

   _____

3. Why should you visit the doctor every year?

   _____

4. What will the doctor measure at your visit?

   _____

   _____

5. What does the doctor listen to?

   _____

6. Why are some people afraid to see the doctor?

   _____

Read the story. Then, answer the questions.

The Desert

When you think of the desert, you may picture lots of sand and not much else. There is more life in the desert than you might think. Many types of cacti grow there. Birds called roadrunners chase lizards through the sand. The desert can be very hot during the daytime, but it gets very cold at night. When the wind blows strongly, it builds large mounds of sand. If you go to the desert, be sure to take enough water. There are not many bodies of water, and it hardly ever rains. You also should wear light clothing, a hat, and plenty of sunscreen.

1. What is the main idea of this story?
    a. Roadrunners chase lizards through the sand.
    b. The desert has plants, animals, and very little rain.
    c. Take a hat and wear sunscreen.

2. What does a cactus look like?
    a. It has sharp, pointed leaves that can hurt you.
    b. It has wide, green leaves and needs lots of water.
    c. It produces different kinds of nuts.

3. What do roadrunners do in the desert?

   _____

4. What is the weather like at night in the desert?

   _____

5. Why should you take water to the desert?

   _____

   _____

6. What should you wear to visit the desert?

   _____

Read the story. Then, answer the questions.

The Beach

Have you ever been to the beach? It is fun to play in the sand and then wash off in the water. Tiny fish might tickle your feet when you walk into the ocean. Birds called pelicans fly in circles above the water. When they see a fish move, they dive to catch it. Crabs hurry along the shoreline. You may find seashells in the sand. If you go to a harbor, you will see ships as well as seagulls. The gulls like to eat food that people have thrown away. They are nature's garbage collectors!

1. What is the main idea of this story?
    a. There is a lot to see at the beach.
    b. Crabs hurry along the shoreline.
    c. Seagulls like to eat trash.

2. What can you do at the beach?

    _____

3. Why do pelicans fly in circles?

    _____

    _____

4. What other animals might you find at the beach?

    _____

5. What does the word *harbor* mean?
    a. nature's garbage collectors
    b. a type of seagull
    c. a place where ships unload their goods

6. What do gulls like to eat?

    _____

Read the story. Then, answer the questions.

How Plants Grow

Plants need food, water, and sunlight to grow. After you plant a seed in the dirt, a tiny growth pushes its way out. The plant grows upward, trying to reach the sunlight. After it breaks through the earth, it starts growing taller. The plant must get water, or it can dry out and die. If there is little rain where you live, you may need to water your plant. Plants receive food from the soil. If the soil in your area is poor, you may need to add special food so that the plant gets everything it needs. Some plants bloom into flowers. Others produce nuts. These nuts become the new seeds, and the steps start all over again.

1. What is the main idea of this story?
   a. A plant can die without water.
   b. Plants need food, water, and sunlight.
   c. The steps start all over again.

2. What happens after you plant a seed?

   _____

3. Why do plants grow upward?

   _____

4. When might you need to water your plant?

   _____

5. When might you need to give your plant special food?

   _____

6. What happens after plants produce nuts?

   _____

   _____

Name _____

Read the story. Then, answer the questions.

Animal Babies

Most people have seen a kitten or a puppy. But have you ever seen a baby kangaroo? A baby kangaroo is called a joey. When it is born, it is only about 0.79 inch (2 centimeters) long and weighs about 0.04 ounce (1 gram). It lives in its mother's pouch until it is bigger. A baby koala also lives in its mother's pouch for several months. After it leaves the pouch, the baby koala rides on its mother's back until it can walk easily. Like humans, animal babies learn from their parents. Lion cubs learn how to hunt. Swallows learn how to fly. Ducklings learn how to paddle their feet. They all must learn to live safely on their own.

1. What is the main idea of this story?
   a. Lion cubs learn how to hunt.
   b. A baby kangaroo is called a joey.
   c. Animal babies grow and learn about life.

2. How big is a baby kangaroo when it is born?

   _____

3. How are baby kangaroos and baby koalas alike?

   _____

   _____

4. How are human babies like animal babies?

   _____

5. What do ducklings learn from their parents?

   _____

6. How do you think a dolphin learns to find food by digging in the ocean floor?

   _____

Read the story. Then, answer the questions.

Woodpeckers

You may have seen a woodpecker in a cartoon. There are many different types of woodpeckers, but they all have strong bills and long, sticky tongues. They like to eat ants, beetles, nuts, and berries. Woodpeckers are famous for the hammering noise that comes from their bills. Woodpeckers use their bills to remove bark from trees. When they uncover bugs, they grab them with their tongues. Woodpeckers have claws on their toes to help them hold on to trees while they are hammering. They also use their bills to send messages to other woodpeckers.

1. What is the main idea of this story?
   a. Woodpeckers use their bills to find food and to make noise.
   b. You may have seen a cartoon woodpecker.
   c. Woodpeckers use hammers to look for bugs.

2. What do woodpeckers like to eat?

   _____

3. How does the woodpecker make its hammering sound?
   a. with its long, sticky tongue
   b. with its strong bill
   c. with the claws on its toes

4. How do woodpeckers find food?

   _____

   _____

5. How do woodpeckers send messages to each other?

   _____

Read the story. Then, answer the questions.

Helpful Bugs

Some bugs can destroy crops by eating them. Not all bugs are bad, though. Some bugs even help us. Bees move pollen from one flower to the next. This helps flowers make seeds so that there will be more flowers the next year. Bees also produce honey. Ladybugs are another helpful bug. They eat the bugs that chew on our plants. Finally, spiders may look scary, but they are very helpful bugs. They catch flies, crickets, and moths in their webs. If you find a spider inside the house, ask an adult to help you carefully place it outside. Then, it can do its job.

1. What is the main idea of this story?
    a. Bugs can destroy crops.
    b. Ladybugs are beautiful.
    c. Not all bugs are bad.

2. What do bees produce?
    a. pollen
    b. spiders
    c. honey

3. How do bees help flowers grow?

    _____

    _____

4. How do ladybugs help us?

    _____

5. What do spiders catch in their webs?

    _____

6. What should you do if you find a spider in the house?

    _____

    _____

Name _____

Read the story. Then, answer the questions.

The Water Cycle

All water on the earth is part of the same cycle. Water starts out in oceans, lakes, and streams. When the sun heats the water, water drops rise into the air. Water in this form is called steam. As the air cools, the water drops form clouds. When the clouds become too heavy with water, they produce rain, sleet, or snow. The rain falls back to the earth. Some of the water goes into the soil, where it helps the plants grow. Some of the water falls into the ocean. Then, the water cycle begins again. The next time you drink a glass of water, think about where it came from!

1. What is the main idea of this story?
   a. All water on earth moves through a cycle.
   b. Think about where your glass of water came from.
   c. Rain moves water back to the earth.

2. Where does the water cycle begin?

   _____

3. What happens when the sun heats the water up?

   _____

4. When do water drops form clouds?

   _____

5. What happens when clouds have too much water?

   _____

6. Where does the rain go after it falls back to the earth?

   _____

   _____

Read the story. Then, answer the questions.

Weather

Weather can be wonderful or very frightening. Rain feels nice on a hot day, but too much rain can cause a flood. People can lose their cars and homes, and sometimes their lives. A gentle breeze feels good on your skin, but a strong wind can form a tornado, or twister. A tornado can rip the roof off a house. Snow can be fun to play in, but you cannot travel through a snowstorm. If you see a news report that the weather is going to be dangerous, do not be hasty to go outside and watch. It is more fun to watch the weather on TV than to be caught in it!

1. What is the main idea of this story?
   a. You should watch the weather report on the news.
   b. Snow can be fun to play in.
   c. Weather can be wonderful or frightening.

2. What happens when it rains too much?

   _____

3. Why is *twister* a good name for a tornado?

   _____

   _____

4. What can a tornado do to a house?

   _____

5. What is hard to do in a snowstorm?

   _____

6. What should you do if the news says the weather is going to be dangerous?

   _____

Read the story. Then, answer the questions.

Whales

You may think that whales are just very large fish. But, whales are really more like humans. Whales are mammals. They are warm-blooded, give milk to their babies, and breathe with lungs instead of gills. Whales breathe through an opening on top of their heads, called a blowhole. They breathe out so hard that it produces a jet of mist. The blue whale is the largest animal living today. It can grow to be over 100 feet (30.5 meters) long and weigh up to 150 tons (36,078 kilograms). Although whales are large, there is no need to worry about becoming a whale's snack. Whales eat fish and very tiny animals called plankton.

1. What is the main idea of this story?
   a. Whales are very large mammals.
   b. Whales eat tiny animals.
   c. The blue whale is over 100 feet long.

2. How are whales and humans alike?

   _____

   _____

3. Why is the opening in a whale's head called a *blowhole*?

   _____

4. What is the largest animal living today?

   _____

5. What are *plankton*?
   a. fish
   b. blue whales
   c. tiny animals

6. What do whales eat?

   _____

Name _____

Read the story. Then, answer the questions.

The Moon

The moon lights up the night sky. It takes 24 hours to travel around Earth, so you cannot see it in the daytime. Sometimes the moon looks narrow, and sometimes it looks round. The appearance of the moon has to do with the position of the sun. If the sun and moon are on the same side of Earth, the moon looks dark. This is called a new moon. If the sun and moon are on different sides of Earth, the moon looks round. This is called a full moon. In the middle of these two periods, half the moon is lit, and half is dark. It takes about a month to finish the whole cycle.

1. What is the main idea of this story?
    a. The moon looks different throughout the month.
    b. The moon travels around Earth.
    c. The moon can look thin or fat.

2. Why can you not see the moon in the daytime?

    _____

3. What makes the moon's appearance change?

    _____

4. When does a new moon happen?

    _____

    _____

5. When does a full moon happen?

    _____

    _____

6. How long does it take for the moon to finish one cycle?

    _____

Read the story. Then, answer the questions.

Types of Shelter

Shelter is a basic human need. People have always built shelter. The type of shelter a group built depended on their needs, the climate, and the materials that were available. Some groups moved around a lot. The people in these groups needed to have homes that they could take with them. Other people who lived in cold places had to build their shelter from ice and snow. All of the groups' shelters served the same purpose of protecting the people who lived in them.

1. What is the main idea of this story?
   a. Shelter is a basic human need that comes in many forms.
   b. Building shelter out of ice is easy.
   c. Different groups had different purposes for shelter.

2. Which two words mean the same thing?
   a. ice and mud
   b. shelter and house
   c. basic and need

3. Why would different groups' shelters look different from each other?

   _____

   _____

4. Who needed homes they could take with them?

   _____

5. What purpose does shelter serve?

   _____

6. How might the shelter of someone living in a desert be different from the shelter of someone living in a snowy place?

   _____

Read the story. Then, answer the questions.

The Right to Vote

Have you ever voted for class president? Maybe your class has cast votes for the best movie star or type of ice cream. Voting for members of the government is very important. In the United States and Canada, you have to be 18 to vote in one of these elections. Not everyone has been able to vote in the past. In the United States, women were not allowed to vote until 1920. A special law was passed in 1965 to make sure that all adults get to vote. When you vote, you have a say in who serves in the government and what kinds of laws they pass. Some people say that voting is the most important thing that people can do.

1. What is the main idea of this story?
    a. Chocolate ice cream is the best.
    b. Not everyone can vote in the United States.
    c. Voting is an important thing for people to be able to do.

2. Who can vote in the United States and Canada?

    _____

3. What happens in an *election*?
    a. People cast votes.
    b. People have to be 18.
    c. People pass laws.

4. When were U.S. women first allowed to vote?

    _____

5. What happened in the United States after a special law was passed in 1965?

    _____

6. Why is voting important?

    _____

Read the story. Then, answer the questions.

The U.S. Government

The United States' national government has three branches, or parts. The president leads the country, makes sure that people follow the law, and meets with leaders from other nations. Congress makes laws that apply to people all over the country. Congress has two parts: the Senate and the House of Representatives. The Supreme Court is made up of nine judges who review the laws that Congress passes. Each branch of government has some power over the other two. This means that no one branch can be too powerful. This system of government has worked for over 200 years!

1. What is the main idea of this story?
   a. There are nine judges on the Supreme Court.
   b. The national government has worked for 200 years.
   c. The U.S. government has three parts that have different powers.

2. What does the president of the United States do?

   _____

   _____

3. What does Congress do?

   _____

   _____

4. How many judges serve on the Supreme Court?

   _____

5. Why is it important that no branch be too powerful?

   _____

Read the story. Then, answer the questions.

Continents

Earth has seven continents: Africa, Antarctica, Asia, Australia, Europe, South America, and North America. All of these continents used to make up one big continent, but over thousands of years the land split. Huge pieces of land drifted apart. The oceans filled in the spaces between the pieces of land. The continents we know today were the result. Each continent looks different and has different plants, animals, and weather than the others. North America does not have tigers, but Asia does. Antarctica does not have a jungle, but South America does. The continents do have similarities too. Some of these similarities seem to be because the seven continents used to be one big piece of land.

1. What is the main idea of this story?
   a. Earth is made of land and water.
   b. Earth has seven continents, which used to be one piece of land.
   c. Earth has many types of animals, plants, and weather.

2. List the seven continents.

   _____

   _____

3. How long did it take for the continents to form?

   _____

4. How are the continents different?

   _____

5. Which type of land can you find in South America?

   _____

6. Why might continents with an ocean between them have similarities?

   _____

Read the story. Then, answer the questions.

The Liberty Bell

A giant bell called the Liberty Bell stands for freedom in the United States. It measures 30 feet (10 meters) high and 12 feet (3.7 meters) around. The bell was rung in 1776 to call people to hear the Declaration of Independence. This speech told them that the American colonies were breaking away from England to form their own country. The bell has a large crack in it, so it cannot be used anymore. The last time the Liberty Bell was rung was in 1846. Today, the bell stands in Independence Hall in Philadelphia, Pennsylvania. Even though the bell cannot be rung any longer, it still reminds Americans of the people who fought so their country could be free.

1. What is the main idea of this story?
   a. The Liberty Bell stands for freedom.
   b. People fought so they could be free.
   c. The Americans broke away to form their own country.

2. What does the Liberty Bell look like?

   _____

   _____

3. Why was the bell rung in 1776?

   _____

4. Where is the Liberty Bell today?

   _____

5. When was the Liberty Bell last rung?

   _____

6. What does the Liberty Bell remind Americans of?

   _____

Name _____

Read the story. Then, answer the questions.

Coming to North America

For over 200 years, people from other countries have wanted to come to North America. Many travelers from England and France settled in the northeastern part of North America before the United States was formed. Often, they lived in areas that reminded them of home. Many people from northern Europe ended up in what is now the northern part of the United States and Canada. Others from warmer countries settled farther south. Some people came because they wanted to go to a different type of church than the one their country's government wanted them to. Others came because they had little food or work back home. Travelers to North America were able to start new lives.

1. What is the main idea of this story?
    a. Many settlers traveled south.
    b. People from Europe came to North America.
    c. Europe has people from many different countries.

2. How long have people from other countries been coming to North America?

    _____

3. Who settled in the northeastern part of North America before the United States was formed?

    _____

    _____

4. Why did people come to the United States?

    _____

    _____

5. What do you think the trip from Europe to North America was like?

    _____

    _____

Read the story. Then, answer the questions.

Going West

As more people moved to the new nation of the United States, people wanted more room. They wanted to raise their families on land that was clean and open. Many decided to move west and traveled in groups of covered wagons. Dusty trail life brought new dangers: snakes, wolves, and robbers. The weather could be very hot or very cold. Many died along the trail. Some people made it all the way to the coast of California. A lucky few found gold in the rivers and mountains there. People who moved west from the eastern United States probably had a strong spirit of adventure.

1. What is the main idea of this story?
   a. More people should move to the western United States.
   b. People in the United States wanting something different moved west.
   c. City life is better than life on a farm.

2. Why did people start moving out of cities in the eastern United States?

   _____

   _____

3. How did many people travel to the west?

   _____

4. What dangers did trail life bring?

   _____

5. What did a few people find in California?

   _____

6. What were the people who moved west like?

   _____

Read the story. Then, answer the questions.

Railroads

People may not use railroads much today, but they play an important part in history. For centuries, railroads have helped carry people and goods long distances. In the United States, travel was much harder before a railroad tied together the eastern and western parts of the country. Workers in the eastern United States built a railroad heading west. A different crew in the west started building a railroad heading east. In 1869, the two lines met in the state of Utah. The crews hammered in a special golden nail to tie the two tracks together. After that, people could travel from one coast of the United States to the other! The next time you have to stop at a railroad crossing to let a train go by, think about how important railways have been in history.

1. What is the main idea of this story?
    a. Railroads have an important history in the United States.
    b. No one uses railroads today.
    c. You have to stop to let trains go by.

2. Why was traveling harder before the railroads were built?

    _____

3. Where did the two railroads begin?

    _____

4. Where did the two lines meet?

    _____

5. Why did the crews use a golden nail?

    _____

    _____

6. Why do more people still not travel across the United States on a train?

    _____

Read the story. Then, answer the questions.

Cities and Towns

Do you know the difference between a city and a town? In general, a city is much larger. In a town, you may have only one school that everyone your age goes to. A city may have many schools for people of the same age. They may have sports teams that play each other for a city title. In a town, you may know most of the other people living there. In a city, you may know only the people on your block or in your building. A city may have more money to provide services, but more people are trying to use those services. There are good and bad things about living in either place.

1. What is the main idea of this story?
   a. Cities are better for young people to live in.
   b. There are good and bad things about life in a town or a city.
   c. People in towns never have any money.

2. How are schools different in cities and towns?

   _____

   _____

3. Who might you know in a town?

   _____

4. Who might you know in a city?

   _____

5. What are some good and bad things about living in a town?

   _____

   _____

Read the story. Then, answer the questions.

Building a Community

A community is a group of people who care about each other. A community might include your neighbors, school, sports teams, or clubs. People will often offer to help others in their communities. You can be useful to each other. You might decide to walk your neighbor's dog or go to the store for your grandmother. Your uncle might watch your cat while your family goes on vacation. A family down the street might ask you if you want to go to the movies. It is important for people to feel like part of a community. Always be kind and thoughtful to the people in your community, even if you do not know their names.

1. What is the main idea of this story?
    a. Your neighbor might ask you to walk his dog.
    b. Everyone likes being in a community.
    c. A community is made up of people who care about each other.

2. What people might a community include?

    _____

3. How might you help someone in your community?

    _____

4. How might someone in your community help you?

    _____

5. How should you treat people in your community?

    _____

6. Why do people like to feel they are part of a community?

    _____

    _____

Name _____

Read the story.

Brad and Amy

Brad and Amy are brother and sister. They both like playing sports. Brad is on the soccer team. "Soccer is better than any other sport," Brad says. Amy likes basketball. She plays at the park down the street. Brad and Amy have a little brother named Steve. Steve would rather read a good book than play sports. He does like to watch his brother and sister play, though. He sits on the sidelines and claps for them. They are both good at their sports!

Decide whether each sentence is a fact (F) or an opinion (O).

_____ Brad is on the soccer team.

_____ Soccer is better than any other sport.

_____ Amy plays basketball at the park.

_____ Steve is Brad and Amy's little brother.

_____ Brad and Amy are both good at their sports.

_____ Steve sits and claps for his brother and sister.

Write a fact from the story.

_____

_____

Write an opinion from the story.

_____

_____

Read the story.

Making Baskets

Today in art class, we made baskets for our mothers. My basket was the best. I put flowers inside of it. I painted the basket purple. Purple is the prettiest color. Then, I drew a picture of my brothers and me. I wrote a note that said "I love you, Mom." She will love it. Next, I will make a basket for my father. His birthday is next week!

Decide whether each sentence is a fact (F) or an opinion (O).

_____ We made baskets in art class.

_____ My basket was the best.

_____ Purple is the prettiest color.

_____ I drew a picture of my brothers.

_____ Mom will love the basket.

_____ My father's birthday is next week.

Write a fact from the story.

_____

_____

Write an opinion from the story.

_____

_____

Name _____

Read the story.

Dogs and Cats

Dogs come in many different sizes. We have two small dogs and one big one. The big dog is the sweetest. He runs to the door when I come home from school. Then, he licks my hand. He likes to chase balls in the yard. My friend Cara thinks cats are smarter than dogs. Her cat had kittens last summer. Kittens may be cute, but dogs are better pets than cats.

Decide whether each sentence is a fact (F) or an opinion (O).

_____ We have three dogs.

_____ My big dog runs to the door.

_____ He likes to chase balls.

_____ Cats are smarter than dogs.

_____ Cara's cat had kittens.

_____ Dogs are better pets than cats.

Write a fact from the story.

_____

_____

Write an opinion from the story.

_____

_____

Read the story.

Winter Fun

Some people like spring, but not me. Winter is the best season. My family goes to the mountains every year. My stepmom is a good skier. She will ski while we watch. My dad wears snowshoes and goes on long hikes. My brothers and I like to make people out of snow. The nights are too cold to be outside, but we stay warm in our cabin. My stepmom makes us hot cocoa at bedtime, and we tell stories.

Decide whether each sentence is a fact (F) or an opinion (O).

_____ Winter is the best season.

_____ My family goes to the mountains.

_____ My stepmom is a good skier.

_____ Dad goes on long hikes.

_____ The nights are too cold.

_____ My stepmom makes us hot cocoa.

Write a fact from the story.

_____

_____

Write an opinion from the story.

_____

_____

Read the story.

My Funny Uncle

Uncle Larry is very funny. He tells stories about his life in the circus. He was a famous clown when he was young. He wears silly masks and tells the best jokes. He can make me laugh. It is hard to get my mother to let me stay up late, but when Uncle Larry is in town, it is easy. She lets me stay up and listen to his stories. Someday, I hope I have funny stories of my own because I know I am funny too.

Decide whether each sentence is a fact (F) or an opinion (O).

_____ Uncle Larry is funny.

_____ He tells stories about the circus.

_____ His jokes are the best.

_____ Uncle Larry can make me laugh.

_____ It is hard to get my mother to let me stay up late.

_____ I am funny too.

Write a fact from the story.

_____

_____

Write an opinion from the story.

_____

_____

Name _____

Read the story.

Drinking Water

Drinking water is more important than eating. Some people drink several glasses of water every day. Water helps your body work like it should. You want to make sure you drink clean water. You will get sick if you drink water that is dirty. Rainwater is not always clean. Many people drink the water from their kitchen sinks. The water from your kitchen sink has been tested and called safe to drink.

Decide whether each sentence is a fact (F) or an opinion (O).

_____ Drinking water is more important than eating.

_____ Some people drink several glasses a day.

_____ Water helps your body work like it should.

_____ You will get sick if you drink dirty water.

_____ Rainwater is not always clean.

_____ The water from your kitchen sink has been tested.

Write a fact from the story.

_____

_____

Write an opinion from the story.

_____

_____

Name _____

Read the story.

I Like Math

Some people think math is hard, but really, it is easy. When my teacher asks someone to go to the board, I raise my hand first. Sometimes, I work extra problems just for fun. My friends ask me for help with their math problems. I explain how to work them differently than the teacher does. My parents are both math teachers. They have shown me all of the tricks I know.

Decide whether each sentence is a fact (F) or an opinion (O).

_____ Math is easy.

_____ I raise my hand first.

_____ Working extra problems is fun.

_____ My friends ask me for help.

_____ My parents teach math.

_____ They show me math tricks.

Write a fact from the story.

_____

_____

Write an opinion from the story.

_____

_____

Name _____

Read the story.

Summer Swimming

Swimming is a great way to cool off in the summer. The pool feels wonderful after being in the hot sun. I like to take a picnic to the pool. I daydream and write in my journal. When I get too hot, I jump back in the water. Sometimes, my brother and his friends come along. They like to stay in the pool all day. When I am not looking, they splash me with cold water! You would think it is cold too after being in the sun.

Decide whether each sentence is a fact (F) or an opinion (O).

_____ Swimming is a great way to cool off.

_____ The pool feels wonderful.

_____ I write in my journal.

_____ I jump back in the water.

_____ My brother and his friends come along.

_____ You would think it is cold too.

Write a fact from the story.

_____

_____

Write an opinion from the story.

_____

_____

Name _____

Read the story.

Learning to Cook

My brother is helping me learn to cook. He is an excellent cook. Last night, we made noodles with tomatoes for dinner. We also made a spinach salad. We were going to make a pie, but we were out of ice cream. Pie without ice cream on the side is not very tasty. Our mother loved the meal. We are even better cooks than she is!

Decide whether each sentence is a fact (F) or an opinion (O).

_____ My brother is an excellent cook.

_____ We made noodles with tomatoes for dinner.

_____ We also made a spinach salad.

_____ We were out of ice cream.

_____ Pie without ice cream is not very tasty.

_____ We are better cooks than our mother.

Write a fact from the story.

_____

_____

Write an opinion from the story.

_____

_____

Read the story.

Oranges

Oranges are the best fruit. They have a bumpy skin and a sweet taste. You can eat them alone or make orange juice out of them. Orange juice tastes better than lemonade with breakfast. Lemonade is better for a snack. Oranges are hard to peel. Mom cuts my oranges into pieces for my lunch. My friends ask if I will trade for either apples or bananas, but I always say no!

Decide whether each sentence is a fact (F) or an opinion (O).

_____ Oranges have a bumpy skin.

_____ You can eat them alone or make juice.

_____ Lemonade is better for a snack.

_____ Oranges are hard to peel.

_____ Mom cuts my oranges into pieces.

_____ My friends ask if I will trade.

Write a fact from the story.

_____

_____

Write an opinion from the story.

_____

_____

Read the story.

Bubbles

My little dog is named Bubbles. We call him that because he tries to eat the soap bubbles in the bath. Bubbles gets a lot of baths because he loves to get dirty. After a rain is the worst. He rolls in the mud. Then, he runs from us as we chase him. It looks like he is laughing at us. Mom gets so mad at him! It is hard to stay mad for long. We just start filling up the tub again.

Decide whether each sentence is a fact (F) or an opinion (O).

_____ My dog is named Bubbles.

_____ He tries to eat soap bubbles.

_____ After a rain is the worst.

_____ He runs from us as we chase him.

_____ It is hard to stay mad for long.

_____ We fill up the tub again.

Write a fact from the story.

_____

_____

Write an opinion from the story.

_____

_____

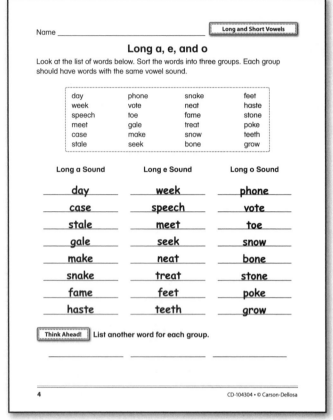

Name _____ Long and Short Vowels

Long a, e, and o

Look at the list of words below. Sort the words into three groups. Each group should have words with the same vowel sound.

day	phone	snake	feet
week	vote	neat	haste
speech	toe	fame	stone
meet	gale	treat	poke
case	make	snow	teeth
stale	seek	bone	grow

Long a Sound	Long e Sound	Long o Sound
day	week	phone
case	speech	vote
stale	meet	toe
gale	seek	snow
make	neat	bone
snake	treat	stone
fame	feet	poke
haste	teeth	grow

Think Ahead! List another word for each group.

_____ _____ _____

4   CD-104304 • © Carson-Dellosa

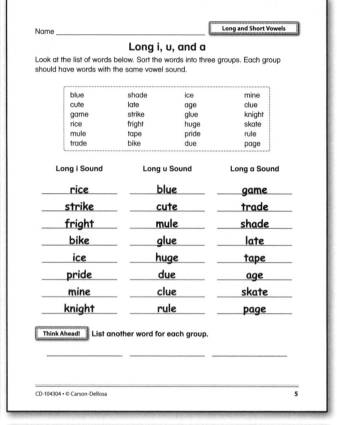

Name _____ Long and Short Vowels

Long i, u, and a

Look at the list of words below. Sort the words into three groups. Each group should have words with the same vowel sound.

blue	shade	ice	mine
cute	late	age	clue
game	strike	glue	knight
rice	fright	huge	skate
mule	tape	pride	rule
trade	bike	due	page

Long i Sound	Long u Sound	Long a Sound
rice	blue	game
strike	cute	trade
fright	mule	shade
bike	glue	late
ice	huge	tape
pride	due	age
mine	clue	skate
knight	rule	page

Think Ahead! List another word for each group.

_____ _____ _____

CD-104304 • © Carson-Dellosa   5

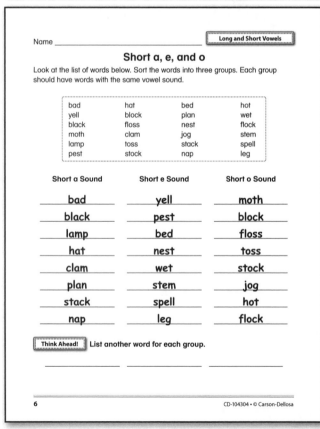

Name _____ Long and Short Vowels

Short a, e, and o

Look at the list of words below. Sort the words into three groups. Each group should have words with the same vowel sound.

bad	hat	bed	hot
yell	block	plan	wet
black	floss	nest	flock
moth	clam	jog	stem
lamp	toss	stack	spell
pest	stock	nap	leg

Short a Sound	Short e Sound	Short o Sound
bad	yell	moth
black	pest	block
lamp	bed	floss
hat	nest	toss
clam	wet	stock
plan	stem	jog
stack	spell	hot
nap	leg	flock

Think Ahead! List another word for each group.

_____ _____ _____

6   CD-104304 • © Carson-Dellosa

Name _____ Long and Short Vowels

Short i, u, and a

Look at the list of words below. Sort the words into three groups. Each group should have words with the same vowel sound.

dust	drip	map	truck
quick	hand	rap	bun
trip	sack	club	win
quack	stuff	lip	pass
thumb	dish	cab	lunch
fist	fact	must	clip

Short i Sound	Short u Sound	Short a Sound
quick	dust	quack
trip	thumb	hand
fist	stuff	sack
drip	club	fact
dish	must	map
lip	truck	rap
win	bun	cab
clip	lunch	pass

Think Ahead! List another word for each group.

_____ _____ _____

CD-104304 • © Carson-Dellosa   7

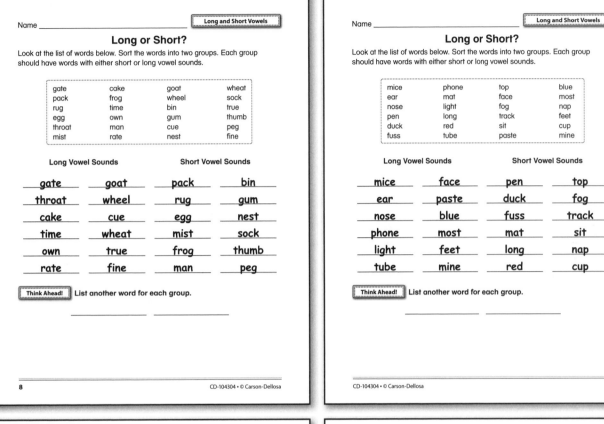

Name _____   **Long and Short Vowels**

Long or Short?

Look at the list of words below. Sort the words into two groups. Each group should have words with either short or long vowel sounds.

gate	cake	goat	wheat
pack	frog	wheel	sock
rug	time	bin	true
egg	own	gum	thumb
throat	man	cue	peg
mist	rate	nest	fine

Long Vowel Sounds

gate	goat
throat	wheel
cake	cue
time	wheat
own	true
rate	fine

Short Vowel Sounds

pack	bin
rug	gum
egg	nest
mist	sock
frog	thumb
man	peg

Think Ahead!   List another word for each group.

_____   _____

8   CD-104304 • © Carson-Dellosa

Name _____   **Long and Short Vowels**

Long or Short?

Look at the list of words below. Sort the words into two groups. Each group should have words with either short or long vowel sounds.

mice	phone	top	blue
ear	mat	face	most
nose	light	fog	nap
pen	long	track	feet
duck	red	sit	cup
fuss	tube	paste	mine

Long Vowel Sounds

mice	face
ear	paste
nose	blue
phone	most
light	feet
tube	mine

Short Vowel Sounds

pen	top
duck	fog
fuss	track
mat	sit
long	nap
red	cup

Think Ahead!   List another word for each group.

_____   _____

CD-104304 • © Carson-Dellosa   9

Name _____   **R-Controlled Vowels**

ar, er, and ir

Look at the words in the list below. Sort the words into three groups. Each group should have words with ar, er, or ir.

govern	barn	herd	park
mark	first	squirm	danger
dart	serve	arm	circle
squirrel	swimmer	certain	dirt
bird	perhaps	firm	hard
jar	chirp	herself	cart

ar Sound

mark
dart
jar
barn
arm
park
hard
cart

er Sound

govern
serve
swimmer
perhaps
herd
certain
herself
danger

ir Sound

squirrel
bird
first
chirp
squirm
firm
circle
dirt

Think Ahead!   Write a sentence that includes three of these words.

_____

10   CD-104304 • © Carson-Dellosa

Name _____   **R-Controlled Vowels**

ur, ar, and _____

Look at the words in the list below. Sort the words with ur or ar into the first two groups. Look at the letters of the remaining words and label a third group. Write the words that belong in each group.

burr	artist	feather	return
power	part	shark	dancer
hunger	card	center	furry
turn	purpose	yard	farm
super	surprise	suffer	yarn
start	century	writer	slurp

ur Sound

burr
turn
purpose
surprise
century
return
furry
slurp

ar Sound

start
artist
part
card
shark
yard
farm
yarn

er Sound

power
hunger
super
feather
center
suffer
writer
dancer

Think Ahead!   Write a sentence that includes three of these words.

_____

CD-104304 • © Carson-Dellosa   11

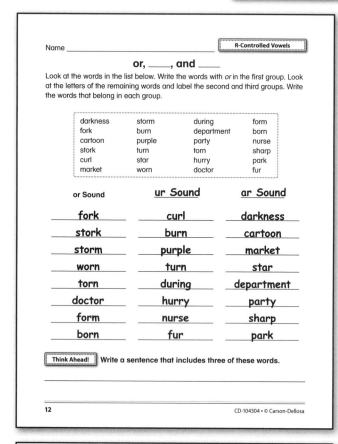

Name _____   R-Controlled Vowels

or, _____, and _____

Look at the words in the list below. Write the words with *or* in the first group. Look at the letters of the remaining words and label the second and third groups. Write the words that belong in each group.

darkness	storm	during	form
fork	burn	department	born
cartoon	purple	party	nurse
stork	turn	torn	sharp
curl	star	hurry	park
market	worn	doctor	fur

or Sound	ur Sound	ar Sound
fork	curl	darkness
stork	burn	cartoon
storm	purple	market
worn	turn	star
torn	during	department
doctor	hurry	party
form	nurse	sharp
born	fur	park

Think Ahead! Write a sentence that includes three of these words.

_____

12   CD-104304 • © Carson-Dellosa

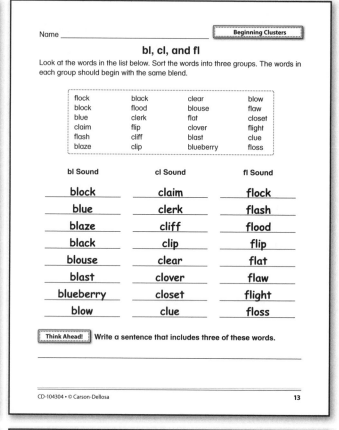

Name _____   Beginning Clusters

bl, cl, and fl

Look at the words in the list below. Sort the words into three groups. The words in each group should begin with the same blend.

flock	black	clear	blow
block	flood	blouse	flaw
blue	clerk	flat	closet
claim	flip	clover	flight
flash	cliff	blast	clue
blaze	clip	blueberry	floss

bl Sound	cl Sound	fl Sound
block	claim	flock
blue	clerk	flash
blaze	cliff	flood
black	clip	flip
blouse	clear	flat
blast	clover	flaw
blueberry	closet	flight
blow	clue	floss

Think Ahead! Write a sentence that includes three of these words.

_____

CD-104304 • © Carson-Dellosa   13

Name _____   Beginning Clusters

gl, pl, and sl

Look at the words in the list below. Sort the words into three groups. The words in each group should begin with the same blend.

glove	pleasure	slip	glass
please	plop	slate	plus
pluck	glance	sleek	slide
sleep	place	glow	player
plentiful	gleam	slope	glue
glad	slow	gloom	slim

gl Sound	pl Sound	sl Sound
glove	please	sleep
glad	pluck	slow
glance	plentiful	slip
gleam	pleasure	slate
glow	plop	sleek
gloom	place	slope
glass	plus	slide
glue	player	slim

Think Ahead! Write a sentence that includes three of these words.

_____

14   CD-104304 • © Carson-Dellosa

Name _____   Beginning Clusters

sh, sk, and st

Look at the words in the list below. Sort the words into three groups. The words in each group should begin with the same blend.

storm	share	skill	skip
shave	stink	sky	short
shovel	skate	shall	stale
skunk	shiver	skirt	stomach
stair	ski	steak	steam
skin	shirt	steep	shade

sh Sound	sk Sound	st Sound
shave	skunk	storm
shovel	skin	stair
share	skate	stink
shiver	ski	steak
shirt	skill	steep
shall	sky	stale
short	skirt	stomach
shade	skip	steam

Think Ahead! Write a sentence that includes three of these words.

_____

CD-104304 • © Carson-Dellosa   15

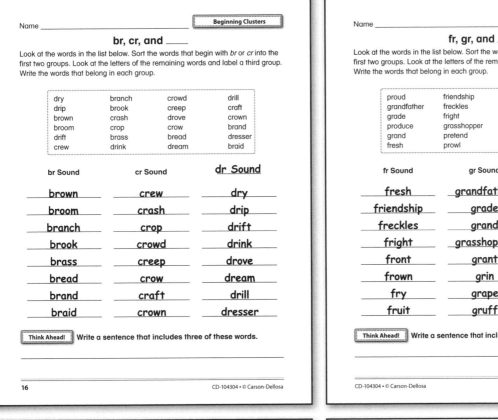

Name _____   **Beginning Clusters**

br, cr, and _____

Look at the words in the list below. Sort the words that begin with *br* or *cr* into the first two groups. Look at the letters of the remaining words and label a third group. Write the words that belong in each group.

dry	branch	crowd	drill
drip	brook	creep	craft
brown	crash	drove	crown
broom	crop	crow	brand
drift	brass	bread	dresser
crew	drink	dream	braid

br Sound	cr Sound	dr Sound
brown	crew	dry
broom	crash	drip
branch	crop	drift
brook	crowd	drink
brass	creep	drove
bread	crow	dream
brand	craft	drill
braid	crown	dresser

Think Ahead! Write a sentence that includes three of these words.

_____

    CD-104304 • © Carson-Dellosa

Name _____   **Beginning Clusters**

fr, gr, and _____

Look at the words in the list below. Sort the words that begin with *fr* or *gr* into the first two groups. Look at the letters of the remaining words and label a third group. Write the words that belong in each group.

proud	friendship	grant	frown
grandfather	freckles	problem	fry
grade	fright	preen	grape
produce	grasshopper	grin	fruit
grand	pretend	pride	promise
fresh	prowl	front	gruff

fr Sound	gr Sound	pr Sound
fresh	grandfather	proud
friendship	grade	produce
freckles	grand	pretend
fright	grasshopper	prowl
front	grant	problem
frown	grin	preen
fry	grape	pride
fruit	gruff	promise

Think Ahead! Write a sentence that includes three of these words.

_____

CD-104304 • © Carson-Dellosa

Name _____   **Beginning Clusters**

str, thr, and _____

Look at the words in the list below. Sort the words that begin with *str* or *thr* into the first two groups. Look at the letters of the remaining words and label a third group. Write the words that belong in each group.

trouble	strike	through	trail
strange	trend	strength	throne
thread	throughout	treat	tryout
throw	straw	three	struggle
stream	trash	threw	street
trio	throat	triangle	strawberry

str Sound	thr Sound	tr Sound
strange	thread	trouble
stream	throw	trio
strike	throughout	trend
straw	throat	trash
strength	through	treat
struggle	three	triangle
street	threw	trail
strawberry	throne	tryout

Think Ahead! Write a sentence that includes three of these words.

_____

    CD-104304 • © Carson-Dellosa

Name _____   **Beginning Clusters**

qu, _____, and _____

Look at the words in the list below. Write the words that begin with *qu* in the first group. Look at the letters of the remaining words and label the second and third groups. Write the words that belong in each group.

sweater	quail	squirm	question
quick	sweep	quite	swing
quiet	squash	sway	squeak
quarter	squirrel	swish	squid
sweet	squirt	swallow	squawk
swim	queen	square	quart

qu Sound	sw Sound	squ Sound
quick	sweater	squash
quiet	sweet	squirrel
quarter	swim	squirt
quail	sweep	squirm
queen	sway	square
quite	swish	squeak
question	swallow	squid
quart	swing	squawk

Think Ahead! Write a sentence that includes three of these words.

_____

CD-104304 • © Carson-Dellosa

Name _____   Beginning Clusters

ch, ____, and ____

Look at the words in the list below. Write the words that begin with *ch* in the first group. Look at the letters of the remaining words and label the second and third groups. Write the words that belong in each group.

thirty	charge	snug	thin
chirp	snake	chimney	thirsty
snack	snap	snail	chat
snowball	checkers	sniff	cheek
thick	cherry	thoughtful	thank
chance	third	thousand	snow

ch Sound	sn Sound	th Sound
chirp	snack	thirty
chance	snowball	thick
charge	snake	third
checkers	snap	thoughtful
cherry	snug	thousand
chimney	snail	thin
chat	sniff	thirsty
cheek	snow	thank

Think Ahead! Write a sentence that includes three of these words.

_____

20   CD-104304 • © Carson-Dellosa

Name _____   Ending Clusters

ck, sh, and st

Look at the words in the list below. Sort the words into three groups. The words in each group should end with the same blend.

push	past	fresh	bash
first	pick	test	stock
cash	fish	flock	fast
sock	best	rock	flash
dish	must	clock	deck
mist	quick	dash	coast

ck Sound	sh Sound	st Sound
sock	push	first
pick	cash	mist
quick	dish	past
flock	fish	best
rock	fresh	must
clock	dash	test
stock	bash	fast
deck	flash	coast

Think Ahead! Write a sentence that includes three of these words.

_____

CD-104304 • © Carson-Dellosa   21

Name _____   Ending Clusters

ch, ck, and ____

Look at the words in the list below. Sort the words that end with *ch* or *ck* into the first two groups. Look at the letters of the remaining words and label a third group. Write the words that belong in each group.

stack	pitch	cluck	branch
rich	struck	much	flash
squash	flock	fresh	quack
which	wish	such	dash
click	trash	block	crash
mash	back	itch	batch

ch Sound	ck Sound	sh Sound
rich	stack	squash
which	click	mash
pitch	struck	wish
much	flock	trash
such	back	fresh
itch	cluck	flash
branch	block	dash
batch	quack	crash

Think Ahead! Write a sentence that includes three of these words.

_____

22   CD-104304 • © Carson-Dellosa

Name _____   Ending Clusters

nt, ____, and ____

Look at the words in the list below. Write the words that end with *nt* in the first group. Look at the letters of the remaining words and label the second and third groups. Write the words that belong in each group.

hunt	brand	rent	think
almond	grant	island	dent
spend	pink	giant	ink
drank	paint	wink	talent
mount	stink	hound	yank
command	around	thank	found

nt Sound	nd Sound	nk Sound
hunt	almond	drank
mount	spend	pink
grant	command	stink
paint	brand	wink
rent	around	thank
giant	island	think
dent	hound	ink
talent	found	yank

Think Ahead! Write a sentence that includes three of these words.

_____

CD-104304 • © Carson-Dellosa   23

Synonyms

Name _____

Read the story below. Decide which word in the box below means almost the same thing as each underlined word or phrase in the story. Write your answers below the story.

contests	baking	go	enjoy
unhappy	playground	chilly	

Summer

I like summer. My friends and I play games in the park. The sun is hot, but the pool is cool. We are sad when it is time to leave.

1. **enjoy**

2. **contests**

3. **playground**

4. **baking**

5. **chilly**

6. **unhappy**

7. **go**

Draw a picture to go with the story.

24   CD-104304 • © Carson-Dellosa

Synonyms

Name _____

Read the story below. Decide which word in the box below means almost the same thing as each underlined word or phrase in the story. Write your answers below the story.

several	rest	closest
street	yellow	younger
tunes	pestering	giant

My Best Friend

My best friend's name is Sally. She has blond hair and green eyes. Sally lives down the road from me in a big house. We like to sit in her room and play songs. Sally has some little brothers who are always bothering us.

1. **closest**

2. **yellow**

3. **street**

4. **giant**

5. **rest**

6. **tunes**

7. **several**

8. **younger**

9. **pestering**

Draw a picture to go with the story.

CD-104304 • © Carson-Dellosa   25

Synonyms

Name _____

Read the story below. Decide which word in the box below means almost the same thing as each underlined word or phrase in the story. Write your answers below the story.

slice	cup	mother	super
hotcakes	complete	father	beginning

Eating Breakfast

Every morning, my mom wakes me up for breakfast. I have a glass of juice and a piece of toast. Sometimes my dad makes pancakes with bananas. A balanced breakfast gets the day off to a great start!

1. **mother**

2. **cup**

3. **slice**

4. **father**

5. **hotcakes**

6. **complete**

7. **super**

8. **beginning**

Draw a picture to go with the story.

26   CD-104304 • © Carson-Dellosa

Synonyms

Name _____

Read the story below. Decide which word in the box below means almost the same thing as each underlined word or phrase in the story. Write your answers below the story.

takes	each	bright	pals
neighbor	pretty	stormy	travel

Going to School

My friends and I go to school in different ways. Trey's mother drives him in her black truck. Jan rides the bus with a girl next door. Tara and Miguel walk to school if the weather is nice. I ride my bicycle every day whether it is rainy or sunny!

1. **pals**

2. **travel**

3. **takes**

4. **neighbor**

5. **pretty**

6. **each**

7. **stormy**

8. **bright**

Draw a picture to go with the story.

CD-104304 • © Carson-Dellosa   27

Flying a Kite

Name _____ Synonyms

Read the story below. Decide which word in the box below means almost the same thing as each underlined word or phrase in the story. Write your answers below the story.

| air | lumber | bound | thin |
| rope | high | pasted | youth |

Flying a Kite

When my father was a boy, he flew kites. He and his brother took a ball of string and some narrow wood. They cut the wood into a square. Then, they glued colorful paper on it. Finally, they tied a tail on the kite. The kite would fly up in the sky!

1. youth
2. rope
3. thin
4. lumber
5. pasted
6. bound
7. high
8. air

Draw a picture to go with the story.

Our New Kittens

Name _____ Synonyms

Read the story below. Decide which word in the box below means almost the same thing as each underlined word or phrase in the story. Write your answers below the story.

| pick | large | spotless | box | hop |
| small | vacation | crying | just | states |

Our New Kittens

Over spring break, our cat had kittens. They were tiny, and they made squeaking sounds instead of meows. She licked their faces to keep them clean. They stayed in a basket until they were big enough to jump out. Mom says that we can keep only one. It is hard to decide which one!

1. vacation
2. small
3. crying
4. spotless
5. box
6. large
7. hop
8. states
9. just
10. pick

Draw a picture to go with the story.

Aunt Jill's Farm

Name _____ Synonyms

Read the story below. Decide which word in the box below means almost the same thing as each underlined word or phrase in the story. Write your answers below the story.

| eat | grow | bit | earth | till |
| visit | shoveling | splash | owns | stony |

Aunt Jill's Farm

Aunt Jill has a piece of land in the country. When we go see her, we help her farm the soil. The ground can be rocky, so digging is hard. We plant the seeds and spray them with water. After they get bigger, we can dine on them!

1. owns
2. bit
3. visit
4. till
5. earth
6. stony
7. shoveling
8. splash
9. grow
10. eat

Draw a picture to go with the story.

Dad's Computer

Name _____ Synonyms

Read the story below. Decide which word in the box below means almost the same thing as each underlined word or phrase in the story. Write your answers below the story.

| class | buy | company | work | papers |
| read | produce | house | articles | notes |

Dad's Computer

Dad showed me how to use the computer at his business. I can type letters to my friends. I can look at funny stories on the Internet. I can prepare reports for school too. I wish we could get a computer for our home!

1. work
2. company
3. notes
4. read
5. articles
6. produce
7. papers
8. class
9. buy
10. house

Draw a picture to go with the story.

Name _____

Synonyms

Read the story below. Decide which word in the box below means almost the same thing as each underlined word or phrase in the story. Write your answers below the story.

nightfall	high	trail	hear
bring	notice	pounding	night
happy	woods	run	hound

Jogging with Mom

Mom and I like to <u>jog</u>¹ every <u>evening</u>². We sometimes <u>take</u>³ our <u>dog</u>⁴, Rudy. We turn down a <u>path</u>⁵ and jog through the <u>forest</u>⁶. We <u>see</u>⁷ the <u>tall</u>⁸ trees and <u>listen to</u>⁹ our feet <u>hitting</u>¹⁰ the ground. Being outside at <u>sundown</u>¹¹ makes me feel <u>joyful</u>¹².

1. **run**
2. **night**
3. **bring**
4. **hound**
5. **trail**
6. **woods**
7. **notice**
8. **high**
9. **hear**
10. **pounding**
11. **nightfall**
12. **happy**

Draw a picture to go with the story.

32 CD-104304 • © Carson-Dellosa

Name _____

Antonyms

Read the story below. Rewrite the story by replacing each underlined word with a word from the list that means the opposite.

windy	light	his	he	your
dark	boy	wet	ocean	

My Book

I am writing <u>my</u> book. It is about a <u>girl</u> named Taylor. <u>She</u> has <u>light</u> hair and <u>dark</u> eyes. <u>Her</u> family lives by the <u>desert</u>. It is very <u>dry</u> there and the air is <u>still</u>.

I am writing your book. It is about a boy named Taylor. He has dark hair and light eyes. His family lives by the ocean. It is very wet there and the air is windy.

My Book

CD-104304 • © Carson-Dellosa 33

Name _____

Antonyms

Read the story below. Rewrite the story by replacing each underlined word with a word from the list that means the opposite.

autumn	cold	plant	less
dies	inside	slowly	old

Seasons

I like <u>spring</u> <u>more</u> than other seasons. The leaves are <u>young</u>. The grass <u>grows</u> <u>quickly</u>. We <u>pick</u> flowers for Mom. We go <u>outside</u> and watch the <u>warm</u> rain.

I like autumn less than other seasons. The leaves are old. The grass dies slowly. We plant flowers for Mom. We go inside and watch the cold rain.

34 CD-104304 • © Carson-Dellosa

Name _____

Antonyms

Read the story below. Rewrite the story by replacing each underlined word with a word from the list that means the opposite.

frown	short	slowly	lost	new
dislike	never	yell	sad	

Book Buddies

My friends and I <u>always</u> <u>talk</u> about what we are reading. I am reading a <u>long</u> book about the jungle. It is going <u>quickly</u>. Joe is reading a <u>funny</u> book. We <u>smile</u> a lot when he talks about it. Rita <u>found</u> an <u>old</u> book at her grandparents' house. We all <u>like</u> the books she reads.

My friends and I never yell about what we are reading. I am reading a short book about the jungle. It is going slowly. Joe is reading a sad book. We frown a lot when he talks about it. Rita lost a new book at her grandparents' house. We all dislike the books she reads.

CD-104304 • © Carson-Dellosa 35

Name _____

Antonyms

Read the story below. Rewrite the story by replacing each underlined word with a word from the list that means the opposite.

her	poorly	she	sold	to
sister	woman	dislike	old	

Pat's Car

My brother Pat has a car. He bought it from a man named Chris. Pat's car is new. The car runs smoothly. I like riding in his car.

  My sister Pat has a car. She sold it to a woman named Chris. Pat's car is old. The car runs poorly. I dislike riding in her car.

36 CD-104304 • © Carson-Dellosa

Name _____

Antonyms

Read the story below. Rewrite the story by replacing each underlined word with a word from the list that means the opposite.

sunset	back	few	sit
country	large	summer	evening

Lynn's House

My friend Lynn lives in the city. Lynn has a tiny house with lots of neighbors. My cat and I go see Lynn every winter. In the morning, we like to stand out front. We like to look at the sunrise.

  My friend Lynn lives in the country. Lynn has a large house with few neighbors. My cat and I go see Lynn every summer. In the evening, we like to sit out back. We like to look at the sunset.

CD-104304 • © Carson-Dellosa 37

Name _____

Antonyms

Read the story below. Rewrite the story by replacing each underlined word with a word from the list that means the opposite.

left	lost	sad	nothing
dark	last	quiet	huge

A Special Puppy

Last week, I found a little puppy. He has bright eyes and a loud bark. He is brown with a white dot on his right leg. We first saw him in our backyard. He seemed to be looking for something. The puppy looked happy.

  Last week, I lost a huge puppy. He has dark eyes and a quiet bark. He is brown with a white dot on his left leg. We last saw him in our backyard. He seemed to be looking for nothing. The puppy looked sad.

38 CD-104304 • © Carson-Dellosa

Name _____

Antonyms

Read the story below. Rewrite the story by replacing each underlined word with a word from the list that means the opposite.

few	ran	bottom	right-side-out
under	nobody	slept	late

Opposite Day

Today was opposite day at school. I woke early and walked to class. Everyone wore their pants inside-out. Many people wore their socks over their pants. My teacher even put shoes on the top of her desk!

  Today was opposite day at school. I slept late and ran to class. Nobody wore their pants right-side-out. Few people wore their socks under their pants. My teacher even put shoes on the bottom of her desk!

CD-104304 • © Carson-Dellosa 39

Name _____ | **Antonyms** |

Read the story below. Rewrite the story by replacing each underlined word or phrase with a word or phrase from the list that means the opposite.

stop	scatter	take down	sometimes
leave	packs	up	day
ahead of	breakfast	east	end

Camping

My family <u>often</u> goes camping. We leave after <u>dinner</u> and drive all <u>night</u>. We drive <u>west</u> and watch the sun come <u>down</u> <u>behind</u> us. We <u>arrive</u> where we camp in the afternoon. We <u>put up</u> our tent. We <u>gather</u> wood and <u>start</u> a fire. My family <u>unpacks</u> the rest of our things to <u>begin</u> our trip.

My family sometimes goes camping. We leave after breakfast and drive all day. We drive east and watch the sun come up ahead of us. We leave where we camp in the afternoon. We take down our tent. We scatter wood and stop a fire. My family packs the rest of our things to end our trip.

Name _____ | **Antonyms** |

Read the story below. Rewrite the story by replacing each underlined word with a word from the list that means the opposite.

| strong | rotten | bad | awake |
| forgot | lost | result | poorly |

Janelle's Day

Janelle had a <u>wonderful</u> day. She played a game with a friend and <u>won</u>. She ate <u>fresh</u> fruit. She <u>remembered</u> to take out the trash. She even discovered that a skunk was the <u>cause</u> of a <u>weak</u> smell in her yard! Now Janelle felt <u>sleepy</u>. She will sleep <u>well</u> tonight.

Janelle had a bad day. She played a game with a friend and lost. She ate rotten fruit. She forgot to take out the trash. She even discovered that a skunk was the result of a strong smell in her yard! Now Janelle felt awake. She will sleep poorly tonight.

Name _____ | **Sequencing** |

1. Read the story.

Picnic

My family decided to go on a picnic. I started baking cookies right away. Mom packed bread and meat for sandwiches. Then, Dad put everything in the car. We picked up Grandma.

2. Read the sentences below. Write them in order as they happened in the story.

Mom packed meat and bread.
I baked cookies.
We picked up Grandma.
We decided to go on a picnic.
Dad packed the car.

1. We decided to go on a picnic.
2. I baked cookies.
3. Mom packed meat and bread.
4. Dad packed the car.
5. We picked up Grandma.

3. Draw a line under the best ending for this story.

<u>We all had a good time.</u>
We went to the zoo.
Grandma brought cookies.

Name _____ | **Sequencing** |

1. Read the story.

Writing a Story

My sister and I got out paper and pencils to write a story. First, we thought of a character. Then, we talked about what the character looked like. Next, we thought of something our character could do. Finally, we thought of a good ending.

2. Read the sentences below. Write them in order as they happened in the story.

We thought of a good ending.
We thought of a character.
We decided what our character would do.
We got out paper and pencils.
We talked about the character's looks.

1. We got out paper and pencils.
2. We thought of a character.
3. We talked about the character's looks.
4. We decided what our character would do.
5. We thought of a good ending.

3. Draw a line under the best ending for this story.

Our character had yellow hair.
<u>We read our story to our dad.</u>
We wrote our story with a pencil.

Name _____ | Sequencing |

I. Read the story.

Getting Ready for School

My mom wakes me up for school. I get out of bed and brush my teeth. I put on my shirt and pants. I eat toast and fruit for breakfast. My stepdad makes sure I put my homework in my bag.

2. Read the sentences below. Write them in order as they happened in the story.

I eat toast and fruit.
I put on my shirt.
I put my homework in my bag.
My mom wakes me up.
I brush my teeth.

1. **My mom wakes me up.**

2. **I brush my teeth.**

3. **I put on my shirt.**

4. **I eat toast and fruit.**

5. **I put my homework in my bag.**

3. Draw a line under the best ending for this story.

Then, I catch the bus.
Mom cooks dinner.
Then, I go to sleep.

CD-104304 • © Carson-Dellosa

Name _____ | Sequencing |

I. Read the story.

Birthday Party

Emily turned eight years old last weekend. Today, she had a birthday party. Everyone came at noon. They sang "Happy Birthday" to Emily and ate cake. Then, they played games outside. Some people stayed to sing songs.

2. Read the sentences below. Write them in order as they happened in the story.

Emily turned eight.
They played outside.
They sang and ate cake.
They came to Emily's party.
They sang songs.

1. **Emily turned eight.**

2. **They came to Emily's party.**

3. **They sang and ate cake.**

4. **They played outside.**

5. **They sang songs.**

3. Draw a line under the best ending for this story.

Emily's brother went to the store.
The teacher asked Emily to stay late.
Emily thanked her friends for coming.

CD-104304 • © Carson-Dellosa

Name _____ | Sequencing |

I. Read the story.

A Gift

My teacher is Miss Wong. Our class wanted to give her a gift. Wayne thought a fish in an aquarium would be nice. April wanted to buy a pen. Mario said that we should make her a sign. We liked that idea best. We wrote, "We love you, Miss Wong!"

2. Read the sentences below. Write them in order as they happened in the story.

Wayne wanted to buy a fish.
Mario said to make her a sign.
April wanted to buy a pen.
We wanted to give Miss Wong a gift.
We wrote, "We love you, Miss Wong!"

1. **We wanted to give Miss Wong a gift.**

2. **Wayne wanted to buy a fish.**

3. **April wanted to buy a pen.**

4. **Mario said to make her a sign.**

5. **We wrote, "We love you, Miss Wong!"**

3. Draw a line under the best ending for this story.

Miss Wong was not at school today.
We gave her a pet hamster.
Miss Wong was proud of the sign.

CD-104304 • © Carson-Dellosa

Name _____ | Sequencing |

I. Read the story.

Fruit Salad

Dad taught me how to make fruit salad. We bought the fruit at the store. We washed it in the sink. Dad cut up the apples. Next, he cut up the oranges. Then, he cut up the bananas. We put them in a bowl with grapes and cherries.

2. Read the sentences below. Write them in order as they happened in the story.

We put the fruit in a bowl.
Dad cut up the oranges.
We washed the fruit.
We bought the fruit.
Dad cut up the apples.

1. **We bought the fruit.**

2. **We washed the fruit.**

3. **Dad cut up the apples.**

4. **Dad cut up the oranges.**

5. **We put the fruit in a bowl.**

3. Draw a line under the best ending for this story.

Dad cut up some more apples.
The salad tasted great!
We washed the bananas.

CD-104304 • © Carson-Dellosa

Name _____   Sequencing

I. Read the story.

Painting My Bedroom

Mom said that I could paint my bedroom. She said that she would help me. We borrowed brushes and bought cans of paint. We changed into old clothes. We rubbed the walls with sandpaper. This made them smooth. We painted the walls green and the trim blue.

2. **Read the sentences below. Write them in order as they happened in the story.**

We borrowed brushes.
We rubbed the walls.
We painted the walls and trim.
We changed into old clothes.
Mom said that I could paint my room.

I. __Mom said that I could paint my room.__

2. __We borrowed brushes.__

3. __We changed into old clothes.__

4. __We rubbed the walls.__

5. __We painted the walls and trim.__

3. **Draw a line under the best ending for this story.**

My new room looks great.
I put on my old jeans.
My sister likes the color orange.

48   CD-104304 • © Carson-Dellosa

Name _____   Sequencing

I. Read the story.

Planting a Garden

I help Grandpa plant his summer garden. First, we go to the store to buy seeds. We rake the soil. We dig holes and plant the seeds. Then, we cover the seeds with dirt. We water the seeds so they will grow.

2. **Read the sentences below. Write them in order as they happened in the story.**

We water the seeds.
We rake the soil.
We buy the seeds.
We cover the seeds with dirt.
We plant the seeds.

I. __We buy the seeds.__

2. __We rake the soil.__

3. __We plant the seeds.__

4. __We cover the seeds with dirt.__

5. __We water the seeds.__

3. **Draw a line under the best ending for this story.**

Grandpa buys a lot of seeds.
Soon, we will have vegetables to eat!
We buy a new rake.

CD-104304 • © Carson-Dellosa   49

Name _____   Sequencing

I. Read the story.

Putting on a Play

Tammy was in her class play. She was picked to play the queen. She practiced her lines so that she could remember them. The night of the play arrived. She got dressed like a queen. Her dad, stepmom, and brother came to watch.

2. **Read the sentences below. Write them in order as they happened in the story.**

She got dressed.
She practiced her lines.
Tammy was chosen to play the queen.
The night of the play arrived.
Her family came.

I. __Tammy was chosen to play the queen.__

2. __She practiced her lines.__

3. __The night of the play arrived.__

4. __She got dressed.__

5. __Her family came.__

3. **Draw a line under the best ending for this story.**

Tammy's mother made her a new dress.
Her friend played the king.
The crowd clapped for the actors.

50   CD-104304 • © Carson-Dellosa

Name _____   Sequencing

I. Read the story.

A New School

My family moved to a new town. I went to a new school. A nice teacher met me at the door. She helped me find my classroom. At lunch, I made a new friend named Ana.

2. **Read the sentences below. Write them in order as they happened in the story.**

She helped me find my classroom.
I went to a new school.
My family moved.
I made a new friend.
I met a nice teacher.

I. __My family moved.__

2. __I went to a new school.__

3. __I met a nice teacher.__

4. __She helped me find my classroom.__

5. __I made a new friend.__

3. **Draw a line under the best ending for this story.**

Now, Ana and I are best friends.
My brother is named Dave.
I wore a new skirt on the first day.

CD-104304 • © Carson-Dellosa   51

Page 52

Reading Fiction

Name _____

Read the story. Then, answer the questions.

Heath is a fast runner. He always wins his class race. A new girl came to Heath's class. Her name was Marisa. She was the fastest runner at her old school. Heath wondered if she could run as fast as him. They had a race after school. Heath and Marisa tied! Now they are best friends.

1. What is a good title for this story?
   a. Marisa's Old School
   b. New Friends
   c. First Place

2. What did Heath wonder?
   if Marisa could run as fast as he could

3. What did Heath and Marisa do?
   a. **had a race after school**
   b. **tied**

4. What do Heath and Marisa have in common?
   They are both fast runners.

5. How do you think Heath felt when Marisa came to his class?
   Answers will vary.

52   CD-104304 • © Carson-Dellosa

Page 53

Reading Fiction

Name _____

Read the story. Then, answer the questions.

Ethan liked to stop by Grandma's house after school. She would fix him a snack. One day, Grandma fell and broke her arm. The doctor said that she needed to rest. Grandma came to stay with Ethan and his mom until she felt better. Now, Ethan fixes Grandma a snack every afternoon.

1. What is a good title for this story?
   a. Helping Grandma
   b. Ethan's Snack
   c. Grandma's Doctor

2. What did Ethan like to do?
   stop by Grandma's house after school for a snack

3. What happened to Grandma?
   She fell and broke her arm.

4. Where did Grandma stay while she was hurt?
   with Ethan and his mom

5. Name something else Ethan could do to help Grandma.
   Answers will vary.

CD-104304 • © Carson-Dellosa   53

Page 54

Reading Fiction

Name _____

Read the story. Then, answer the questions.

Kassie wanted a new puppy. Her mom said that she could get a small one. Kassie picked out a tiny gray puppy named Ruff. Ruff liked to eat. He was always hungry. He got bigger and bigger, until he was almost as tall as Kassie. Kassie said, "I thought we got a small dog!" Mom smiled and said, "You will have to grow bigger to take care of him!"

1. What is a good title for this story?
   a. Kassie's Tiny Puppy
   b. Ruff Liked to Eat
   c. A Big Surprise

2. What kind of dog did Mom want Kassie to get?
   a small one

3. What happened to Ruff?
   He got bigger and bigger.

4. What did Mom tell Kassie she would need to do at the end of the story?
   grow bigger to take care of Ruff

5. What are two ways you can take care of a dog?
   Answers will vary.

54   CD-104304 • © Carson-Dellosa

Page 55

Reading Fiction

Name _____

Read the story. Then, answer the questions.

Vanessa's brother Luke is in the army. He visits countries that are far away. He helps people who need food or doctors. One day, Luke surprised Vanessa. She did not know he was home for a break. He came to Vanessa's school wearing his uniform. She was happy to see him standing in the doorway of the lunchroom. Everyone said that she was a lucky girl.

1. What is a good title for this story?
   a. Army Life
   b. Vanessa's Special Treat
   c. Luke's Uniform

2. What are two things that Luke does in the army?
   a. **visits countries that are far away**
   b. **helps people who need food or doctors**

3. Why was Vanessa surprised?
   She did not know Luke was home for a break.

4. What word means the same as *uniform*?
   a. shoes
   b. army
   c. outfit

5. Why did everyone say that Vanessa was a lucky girl?
   Answers will vary.

CD-104304 • © Carson-Dellosa   55

Page 56

Name _____

Read the story. Then, answer the questions.

It was a sunny day. Sarah and her friends played outside at recess. When it was time to go inside, they heard a clap of thunder. All afternoon, they heard the rain outside. Sarah wondered if she would have to catch the bus in the rain. Her umbrella was at home. After school, Sarah and her friends lined up to leave. It was still raining. Sarah put her coat over her head and ran for the bus. She found a way to stay dry after all!

1. What is a good title for this story?
   a. Umbrellas
   b. Catching the Bus
   c. Sarah's Bright Idea

2. What two things did Sarah and her friends hear?

   a. **a clap of thunder**

   b. **the rain outside**

3. What did Sarah wonder?

   if she would have to catch the bus in the rain

4. What did Sarah do to keep dry?

   put her coat over her head

5. What is another way to keep dry without an umbrella?

   Answers will vary.

56   CD-104304 • © Carson-Dellosa

Page 57

Name _____

Read the story. Then, answer the questions.

Jared's mother teaches at his school. Every morning, Jared and his mom ride to school together. One morning, his mom had a cold and could not go to school. Jared called his friend Juan and asked for a ride. Juan lived down the street from Jared. Juan's uncle usually took Juan to school. Juan's uncle was sick too! Jared had an idea. He asked his mom to help him look up the school bus schedule on the World Wide Web. Jared told Juan to meet him at the bus stop in 5 minutes. They rode to school together on the bus.

1. What is a good title for this story?
   a. Jared's Good Idea
   b. Get Well, Jared
   c. Jared and Juan Ride the Train

2. Which two people are sick in the story?

   a. **Jared's mom**

   b. **Juan's uncle**

3. What was Jared's idea?

   to take the bus

4. Where did Jared find the bus schedule?

   the World Wide Web

5. What might have happened if Jared and Juan got to the bus stop in 10 minutes instead of 5 minutes?

   Answers will vary.

CD-104304 • © Carson-Dellosa   57

Page 58

Name _____

Read the story. Then, answer the questions.

Last week, my class took a trip to the zoo. We went to the snake house. Some people were scared, but not me! I knew we were safe. The snakes were behind the glass. We fed peanuts to the baby goats and watched the monkeys swing from branch to branch. Sometimes, my father calls me a monkey, and now I know why! I wanted to ask my gymnastics coach to teach me some tricks I saw the monkeys do.

1. What is a good title for this story?
   a. The Snake House
   b. Monkey See, Monkey Do
   c. Baby Goats

2. What three animals did the children see at the zoo?

   a. **snakes**

   b. **goats**

   c. **monkeys**

3. Why does the writer know they are safe from the snakes?

   The snakes are behind the glass.

4. What does the writer want to do after seeing the monkeys?

   ask his gymnastics coach to teach him monkey tricks

5. Why do you think the writer's father calls him a monkey?

   Answers will vary.

58   CD-104304 • © Carson-Dellosa

Page 59

Name _____

Read the story. Then, answer the questions.

I have a funny cat named Sam. He imagines that he is a dog! He likes to run after balls that jingle. He brings them back when I throw them. He chases his tail. He even growls at the mailman! Sam's best friend is my little brother, Robert. He follows Robert around the house and sleeps on his bed. Robert wants to teach Sam to walk on a leash. We are sure he can learn!

1. What is a good title for this story?
   a. Cat or Dog?
   b. Robert's Best Friend
   c. The Mailman

2. What does Sam imagine?

   that he is a dog

3. What are three things Sam likes to do?

   a. **Three of the following: run after balls, bring**

   b. **them back, chase his tail, growl at mailman,**

   c. **follow Robert around, sleep on Robert's bed**

4. What does Robert want to teach Sam to do?

   walk on a leash

5. What are some other things you can train a pet to do?

   Answers will vary.

CD-104304 • © Carson-Dellosa   59

Page 60

Name _____

Read the story. Then, answer the questions.

Our school has a new club. It meets every Tuesday after school. It is not a sports club. It is not a science club. It is a community club! The club members help our town by cleaning up litter. The members read to older people and visit sick neighbors. The mayor came to the first meeting. She is happy the club is helping others. I want to join the club so that I can be helpful.

1. What is a good title for this story?
   a. Cleaning Up Litter
   b. The Mayor's Letter
   c. The Community Club

2. What is another word for *community*?
   a. neighborhood
   b. sports
   c. science

3. What are three things the club members do?
   a. **clean up litter**
   b. **read to older people**
   c. **visit sick neighbors**

4. Why does the writer want to join the club?
   so he can be helpful

5. What are some other things you can do to help your community?
   Answers will vary.

Page 61

Name _____

Read the story. Then, answer the questions.

My grandpa was a firefighter for a long time. He helped save people from burning houses. Sometimes, he carried people down a ladder. Now, he has a new job. He does not go into burning buildings anymore. Grandpa visits schools to share knowledge about fire safety. He shows them the burn marks on his old jacket. He tells everyone how to stay safe. My grandpa is a hero.

1. What is a good title for this story?
   a. Fire Safety
   b. Grandpa's New Job
   c. An Old Jacket

2. What did Grandpa do at his old job?
   save people from burning houses

3. Why does Grandpa visit schools?
   to share knowledge about fire safety

4. What are two things Grandpa does at the schools he visits?
   a. **shows them the burn marks on his old jacket**
   b. **tells everyone how to stay safe**

5. Why do you think the writer says Grandpa is a hero?
   Answers will vary.

Page 62

Name _____

Read the story. Then, answer the questions.

Brian's little sister Kayce started school this year. They go to the same school. Brian introduced Kayce to his friends at school. His friends thought she was a pleasure to be around. Some of them had little sisters in kindergarten too. They introduced Kayce to their sisters. Kayce was happy to have new friends. She was also happy to have a brother like Brian. She hoped that she could introduce someone to a new friend!

1. What is a good title for this story?
   a. Kayce's Little Friend
   b. New Introductions
   c. Bothering Brian

2. What does Brian do to help Kayce?
   He introduces her to his friends.

3. How did Brian's friends feel about Kayce?
   They thought she was a pleasure to be around.

4. What did Brian and some of his friends have in common?
   They all had little sisters in kindergarten.

5. Why do you think Kayce would like to introduce someone to a new friend?
   Answers will vary.

Page 63

Name _____

Read the story. Then, answer the questions.

Teeth

Teeth are important for chewing food, so you need to take care of your teeth. When you are a child, you have baby teeth. These fall out and are replaced by adult teeth. You can expect to have a full set of 32 teeth one day. Brush your teeth twice a day, in the morning and at bedtime. Also, floss to remove the bits of food that get stuck between your teeth. That way, you will have a healthy smile!

1. What is the main idea of this story?
   a. You can have a healthy smile.
   b. It is important to take care of your teeth.
   c. Adults have more teeth than children.

2. Why should you take care of your teeth?
   so you can chew food

3. What happens to baby teeth?
   They fall out and are replaced by adult teeth.

4. How many teeth do adults have?
   32

5. How often should you brush your teeth?
   a. only at lunchtime
   b. once a week
   c. twice a day

6. How does flossing help keep your teeth healthy?
   It removes bits of food stuck between your teeth.

Sleep

Read the story. Then, answer the questions.

Are you ever sleepy in class? Children need about 10 hours of sleep each night. It is important to be rested for school every morning. If you are tired, you will have trouble paying attention to your teacher. If you have a hard time falling asleep, try reading a book instead of watching TV before bedtime. Go to bed at the same time every night. Ask your family to play soft music to help you get sleepy. Soon, you will be dreaming!

1. What is the main idea of this story?
   a. Getting enough sleep is important for good health.
   b. Reading a book can help you sleep.
   c. You should dream every night.

2. How much sleep do children need?
   about 10 hours each night

3. What might happen at school if you are tired?
   You might have trouble paying attention to your teacher.

4. What can you do instead of watching TV at bedtime?
   read a book

5. When should you go to bed?
   a. 10 P.M.
   b. only when you feel sleepy
   c. at the same time every night

6. What can your family do to help you get sleepy?
   Play soft music.

64   CD-104304 • © Carson-Dellosa

Exercise

Read the story. Then, answer the questions.

Exercising is a great way to take care of your body. It is something the whole family can do together. You should try to exercise for a little while each day. Some fun things to do are running, jumping rope, or walking a dog. You might enjoy playing sports with your friends. Kickball and basketball are good team sports to try. If you start exercising now, you will be used to it when you get older!

1. What is the main idea of this story?
   a. Everyone should exercise each day.
   b. You might like to play basketball.
   c. You should exercise to take care of your body.

2. What is something your whole family can do?
   exercise

3. How often should you exercise?
   a little while each day

4. What are some fun ways to exercise?
   running, jumping rope, walking the dog

5. What is a team sport?
   something you do with your friends, like playing kickball or basketball

6. If you start exercising now, what will happen when you get older?
   You will be used to it when you get older.

CD-104304 • © Carson-Dellosa   65

Talking It Out

Read the story. Then, answer the questions.

Sometimes, our friends can make us angry or hurt our feelings. Instead of fighting with someone who upsets you, try to talk it out. Ask a teacher or another friend to help you talk to each other. Tell them why you are upset. Your friend may be upset about something you said or did too. Listen to their words calmly. After all, you want them to listen to you too! When both of you are done talking, shake hands and forgive each other.

1. What is the main idea of this story?
   a. Talking out a problem is better than fighting.
   b. Ask a teacher to help.
   c. Your friend may be upset too.

2. What should you do if someone upsets you?
   try to talk it out

3. Who can you ask for help?
   a teacher or another friend

4. Why should you listen to your friend's words calmly?
   You want them to listen to you too.

5. What should you do after you are both done talking?
   shake hands and forgive each other

6. What might happen if you get into a fight with someone who made you angry?
   Answers will vary.

66   CD-104304 • © Carson-Dellosa

Wash Your Hands

Read the story. Then, answer the questions.

You have most likely heard your family and teachers tell you to wash your hands. Be sure to use warm water and soap. Rub your hands together for as long as it takes to sing the A-B-Cs. Then, sing the song again while you rinse them. Soap can help kill the germs, or tiny bugs, that make you sick. If you do not wash your hands, you can pass along an illness to a friend. You could also spread the germs to your eyes or mouth if you touch them before washing your hands. Remember to wash your hands!

1. What is the main idea of this story?
   a. Bugs can make you sick.
   b. Rub your hands together.
   c. You should wash your hands with warm water and soap.

2. How long should you rub your hands together?
   as long as it takes to sing the A-B-Cs

3. What does soap do?
   helps kill germs that make you sick

4. What does the word *germs* mean?
   a. kinds of soap
   b. tiny bugs that can make you sick
   c. ways to wash your hands

5. What could happen if you don't wash your hands?
   You could pass along an illness.

6. Why should you not touch your face before washing your hands?
   You could spread the germs to your eyes or mouth.

CD-104304 • © Carson-Dellosa   67

Name _____

Read the story. Then, answer the questions.

Colds

Catching a cold is not fun. You may have red eyes, a sore throat, and a runny nose. You may want to lie in bed all afternoon and sleep. Your voice might sound funny. There are a few things you can do to get better a little faster. First, get plenty of sleep. Your body needs rest to heal itself. Also, drink lots of water or juice. Warm soup is good for you when you are sick too. Most of all, respect your doctor's orders!

1. What is the main idea of this story?
   a. You should lie in bed all afternoon.
   (b) Take care of your body when you have a cold.
   c. Everyone gets sick every now and then.

2. What are some signs of a cold?
   red eyes, a sore throat, a runny nose

3. What might happen to your voice when you have a cold?
   It might sound funny.

4. Why should you get plenty of sleep when you are sick?
   Your body needs rest to heal itself.

5. What should you eat and drink?
   lots of water or juice, warm soup

6. Why should you respect your doctor's orders?
   Answers will vary.

68 CD-104304 • © Carson-Dellosa

Name _____

Read the story. Then, answer the questions.

Food for Thought

What do you like to eat? You may want a candy bar and a soda after school. These foods have a lot of sugar in them. The sugar perks you up, but it wears off quickly. You will feel tired later, when it is time to do your homework. A better snack is a glass of milk and a sandwich. You might have some carrots or grapes too. Your body will thank you for the good snack.

1. What is the main idea of this story?
   (a) Think about what you eat.
   b. Sugar wears off quickly.
   c. Your body will thank you.

2. What do candy bars and soda have in them?
   a lot of sugar

3. What does sugar do to your body?
   perks you up, but wears off quickly

4. What is a good snack after school?
   glass of milk, a sandwich, vegetables, or fruit

5. Which of these foods is a vegetable?
   a. grape
   b. milk
   (c) carrot

6. Why might someone choose a candy bar and a soda after school?
   Answers will vary.

CD-104304 • © Carson-Dellosa 69

Name _____

Read the story. Then, answer the questions.

Healthy Heart and Lungs

Your heart and lungs are important parts of the body. The heart moves blood through the body. Without lungs, you could not breathe. You must exercise to keep your heart and lungs healthy. Your heart starts beating faster when you run fast or jump rope. You may breathe harder too. It is good to make your heart and lungs work harder sometimes. This makes them stronger, and you will also feel healthier. Keeping yourself healthy can be a lifelong practice so that you can have a long life.

1. What is the main idea of this story?
   a. Your heart works harder when you run.
   b. Without lungs, you could not breathe.
   (c) Exercising keeps your heart and lungs healthy.

2. What does the heart do in the body?
   moves blood through the body

3. What do lungs help you do?
   breathe

4. What happens to your heart when you run fast?
   (a) It starts beating faster.
   b. It stops and starts.
   c. It makes you breathe harder.

5. What happens to your lungs when you jump rope?
   You may breathe harder.

6. Why is it good to make your heart work hard sometimes?
   It makes your heart stronger.

70 CD-104304 • © Carson-Dellosa

Name _____

Read the story. Then, answer the questions.

The Five Senses

Most people have five senses: sight, sound, smell, taste, and touch. You see with your eyes. You hear with your ears. You smell with your nose. You taste with your tongue, and you touch with your hands. If you have a cold, your sense of smell might not work right. This makes things taste funny too. You want to protect your senses. Keep sharp objects away from your eyes. Turn down the music before it hurts your ears. Never touch a hot stove with your bare hands.

1. What is the main idea of this story?
   (a) The five senses help you understand the world.
   b. Never listen to loud music.
   c. You smell with your nose and see with your eyes.

2. What are the five senses?
   sight, sound, smell, taste, touch

3. What does your tongue help you do?
   taste things

4. What might happen to your senses when you have a cold?
   Things might smell or taste funny.

5. How can you keep your sense of sight safe?
   Keep sharp objects away from your eyes.

6. Why should you not touch a hot stove?
   You might get burned.

CD-104304 • © Carson-Dellosa 71

Name _____

Read the story. Then, answer the questions.

Going to the Doctor

Your family takes you to the doctor when you are sick. They should also take you when you are well. You should visit the doctor every year to make sure your body is healthy. The doctor will measure how tall you have grown and how much you weigh. She will look at your eyes, ears, and mouth. She will listen to your heart and lungs. Do not be afraid to go to the doctor. She wants you to stay well so that you do not have to see her more often.

1. What is the main idea of this story?
   a. She will see how tall you have grown.
   (b) Going to the doctor can keep you healthy.
   c. The doctor will look at your eyes.

2. When does your family take you to the doctor?
   when you are sick, when you are well

3. Why should you visit the doctor every year?
   to make sure your body is healthy

4. What will the doctor measure at your visit?
   how tall you have grown and how much you weigh

5. What does the doctor listen to?
   your heart and lungs

6. Why are some people afraid to see the doctor?
   Answers will vary.

72   CD-104304 • © Carson-Dellosa

Name _____

Read the story. Then, answer the questions.

The Desert

When you think of the desert, you may picture lots of sand and not much else. There is more life in the desert than you might think. Many types of cacti grow there. Birds called roadrunners chase lizards through the sand. The desert can be very hot during the daytime, but it gets very cold at night. When the wind blows strongly, it builds large mounds of sand. If you go to the desert, be sure to take enough water. There are not many bodies of water, and it hardly ever rains. You also should wear light clothing, a hat, and plenty of sunscreen.

1. What is the main idea of this story?
   a. Roadrunners chase lizards through the sand.
   (b) The desert has plants, animals, and very little rain.
   c. Take a hat and wear sunscreen.

2. What does a cactus look like?
   (a) It has sharp, pointed leaves that can hurt you.
   b. It has wide, green leaves and needs lots of water.
   c. It produces different kinds of nuts.

3. What do roadrunners do in the desert?
   chase lizards

4. What is the weather like at night in the desert?
   cold

5. Why should you take water to the desert?
   There are not many bodies of water, and it hardly ever rains.

6. What should you wear to visit the desert?
   light clothing, a hat, and plenty of sunscreen

CD-104304 • © Carson-Dellosa   73

Name _____

Read the story. Then, answer the questions.

The Beach

Have you ever been to the beach? It is fun to play in the sand and then wash off in the water. Tiny fish might tickle your feet when you walk into the ocean. Birds called pelicans fly in circles above the water. When they see a fish move, they dive to catch it. Crabs hurry along the shoreline. You may find seashells in the sand. If you go to a harbor, you will see ships as well as seagulls. The gulls like to eat food that people have thrown away. They are nature's garbage collectors!

1. What is the main idea of this story?
   (a) There is a lot to see at the beach.
   b. Crabs hurry along the shoreline.
   c. Seagulls like to eat trash.

2. What can you do at the beach?
   play in the sand, wash off in the water

3. Why do pelicans fly in circles?
   to watch for a fish, and then they dive to catch it

4. What other animals might you find at the beach?
   crabs, seashells

5. What does the word harbor mean?
   a. nature's garbage collectors
   b. a type of seagull
   (c) a place where ships unload their goods

6. What do gulls like to eat?
   food that people have thrown away

74   CD-104304 • © Carson-Dellosa

Name _____

Read the story. Then, answer the questions.

How Plants Grow

Plants need food, water, and sunlight to grow. After you plant a seed in the dirt, a tiny growth pushes its way out. The plant grows upward, trying to reach the sunlight. After it breaks through the earth, it starts growing taller. The plant must get water, or it can dry out and die. If there is little rain where you live, you may need to water your plant. Plants receive food from the soil. If the soil in your area is poor, you may need to add special food so that the plant gets everything it needs. Some plants bloom into flowers. Others produce nuts. These nuts become the new seeds, and the steps start all over again.

1. What is the main idea of this story?
   a. A plant can die without water.
   (b) Plants need food, water, and sunlight.
   c. The steps start all over again.

2. What happens after you plant a seed?
   A tiny growth pushes its way out.

3. Why do plants grow upward?
   to reach the sunlight

4. When might you need to water your plant?
   if there is little rain where you live

5. When might you need to give your plant special food?
   if the soil is poor

6. What happens after plants produce nuts?
   The nuts become the new seeds, and the steps start all over again.

CD-104304 • © Carson-Dellosa   75

Name _____ Reading about Science

Read the story. Then, answer the questions.

Animal Babies

Most people have seen a kitten or a puppy. But have you ever seen a baby kangaroo? A baby kangaroo is called a joey. When it is born, it is only about 0.79 inch (2 centimeters) long and weighs about 0.04 ounce (1 gram). It lives in its mother's pouch until it is bigger. A baby koala also lives in its mother's pouch for several months. After it leaves the pouch, the baby koala rides on its mother's back until it can walk easily. Like humans, animal babies learn from their parents. Lion cubs learn how to hunt. Swallows learn how to fly. Ducklings learn how to paddle their feet. They all must learn to live safely on their own.

1. What is the main idea of this story?
   a. Lion cubs learn how to hunt.
   b. A baby kangaroo is called a joey.
   c. Animal babies grow and learn about life.

2. How big is a baby kangaroo when it is born?
   0.79 inch (2 centimeters); 0.04 ounce (1 gram)

3. How are baby kangaroos and baby koalas alike?
   They both live in their mother's pouch until they are bigger.

4. How are human babies like animal babies?
   They both learn from their parents.

5. What do ducklings learn from their parents?
   how to paddle their feet

6. How do you think a dolphin learns to find food by digging in the ocean floor?
   Answers will vary.

Name _____ Reading about Science

Read the story. Then, answer the questions.

Woodpeckers

You may have seen a woodpecker in a cartoon. There are many different types of woodpeckers, but they all have strong bills and long, sticky tongues. They like to eat ants, beetles, nuts, and berries. Woodpeckers are famous for the hammering noise that comes from their bills. Woodpeckers use their bills to remove bark from trees. When they uncover bugs, they grab them with their tongues. Woodpeckers have claws on their toes to help them hold on to trees while they are hammering. They also use their bills to send messages to other woodpeckers.

1. What is the main idea of this story?
   a. Woodpeckers use their bills to find food and to make noise.
   b. You may have seen a cartoon woodpecker.
   c. Woodpeckers use hammers to look for bugs.

2. What do woodpeckers like to eat?
   ants, beetles, nuts, and berries

3. How does the woodpecker make its hammering sound?
   a. with its long, sticky tongue
   b. with its strong bill
   c. with the claws on its toes

4. How do woodpeckers find food?
   They remove the bark from trees and grab bugs with their long, sticky tongues.

5. How do woodpeckers send messages to each other?
   They use their bills to tap on trees.

Name _____ Reading about Science

Read the story. Then, answer the questions.

Helpful Bugs

Some bugs can destroy crops by eating them. Not all bugs are bad, though. Some bugs even help us. Bees move pollen from one flower to the next. This helps flowers make seeds so that there will be more flowers the next year. Bees also produce honey. Ladybugs are another helpful bug. They eat the bugs that chew on our plants. Finally, spiders may look scary, but they are very helpful bugs. They catch flies, crickets, and moths in their webs. If you find a spider inside the house, ask an adult to help you carefully place it outside. Then, it can do its job.

1. What is the main idea of this story?
   a. Bugs can destroy crops.
   b. Ladybugs are beautiful.
   c. Not all bugs are bad.

2. What do bees produce?
   a. pollen
   b. spiders
   c. honey

3. How do bees help flowers grow?
   They move pollen from one flower to the next so that flowers can produce seeds for the next year.

4. How do ladybugs help us?
   They eat the bugs that chew on our plants.

5. What do spiders catch in their webs?
   flies, crickets, and moths

6. What should you do if you find a spider in the house?
   Ask an adult to help you carefully place it outside.

Name _____ Reading about Science

Read the story. Then, answer the questions.

The Water Cycle

All water on the earth is part of the same cycle. Water starts out in oceans, lakes, and streams. When the sun heats the water, water drops rise into the air. Water in this form is called steam. As the air cools, the water drops form clouds. When the clouds become too heavy with water, they produce rain, sleet, or snow. The rain falls back to the earth. Some of the water goes into the soil, where it helps the plants grow. Some of the water falls into the ocean. Then, the water cycle begins again. The next time you drink a glass of water, think about where it came from!

1. What is the main idea of this story?
   a. All water on earth moves through a cycle.
   b. Think about where your glass of water came from.
   c. Rain moves water back to the earth.

2. Where does the water cycle begin?
   in oceans, lakes, and streams

3. What happens when the sun heats the water up?
   Water drops rise into the air as steam.

4. When do water drops form clouds?
   when the air cools

5. What happens when clouds have too much water?
   They produce rain, sleet, or snow.

6. Where does the rain go after it falls back to the earth?
   Some of the water goes into the soil, and some of it falls back into the ocean.

Name _____ **Reading about Science**

Read the story. Then, answer the questions.

Weather

Weather can be wonderful or very frightening. Rain feels nice on a hot day, but too much rain can cause a flood. People can lose their cars and homes, and sometimes their lives. A gentle breeze feels good on your skin, but a strong wind can form a tornado, or twister. A tornado can rip the roof off a house. Snow can be fun to play in, but you cannot travel through a snowstorm. If you see a news report that the weather is going to be dangerous, do not be hasty to go outside and watch. It is more fun to watch the weather on TV than to be caught in it!

1. What is the main idea of this story?
   a. You should watch the weather report on the news.
   b. Snow can be fun to play in.
   c. Weather can be wonderful or frightening.

2. What happens when it rains too much?
   There can be a flood.

3. Why is *twister* a good name for a tornado?
   Answers will vary.

4. What can a tornado do to a house?
   rip the roof off

5. What is hard to do in a snowstorm?
   travel

6. What should you do if the news says the weather is going to be dangerous?
   Stay inside; watch the weather on TV.

Name _____ **Reading about Science**

Read the story. Then, answer the questions.

Whales

You may think that whales are just very large fish. But, whales are really more like humans. Whales are mammals. They are warm-blooded, give milk to their babies, and breathe with lungs instead of gills. Whales breathe through an opening on top of their heads, called a blowhole. They breathe out so hard that it produces a jet of mist. The blue whale is the largest animal living today. It can grow to be over 100 feet (30.5 meters) long and weigh up to 150 tons (36,078 kilograms). Although whales are large, there is no need to worry about becoming a whale's snack. Whales eat fish and very tiny animals called plankton.

1. What is the main idea of this story?
   a. Whales are very large mammals.
   b. Whales eat tiny animals.
   c. The blue whale is over 100 feet long.

2. How are whales and humans alike?
   They are mammals; both are warm-blooded, give milk to their babies, and breathe with lungs.

3. Why is the opening in a whale's head called a *blowhole*?
   The whale blows air and a jet of water through it.

4. What is the largest animal living today?
   blue whale

5. What are *plankton*?
   a. fish
   b. blue whales
   c. tiny animals

6. What do whales eat?
   fish and tiny animals called plankton

Name _____ **Reading about Science**

Read the story. Then, answer the questions.

The Moon

The moon lights up the night sky. It takes 24 hours to travel around Earth, so you cannot see it in the daytime. Sometimes the moon looks narrow, and sometimes it looks round. The appearance of the moon has to do with the position of the sun. If the sun and moon are on the same side of Earth, the moon looks dark. This is called a new moon. If the sun and moon are on different sides of Earth, the moon looks round. This is called a full moon. In the middle of these two periods, half the moon is lit, and half is dark. It takes about a month to finish the whole cycle.

1. What is the main idea of this story?
   a. The moon looks different throughout the month.
   b. The moon travels around Earth.
   c. The moon can look thin or fat.

2. Why can you not see the moon in the daytime?
   It is traveling around Earth.

3. What makes the moon's appearance change?
   the position of the sun

4. When does a new moon happen?
   when the sun and moon are on the same side of Earth

5. When does a full moon happen?
   when the sun and moon are on different sides of Earth

6. How long does it take for the moon to finish one cycle?
   about a month

Name _____ **Reading about Social Studies**

Read the story. Then, answer the questions.

Types of Shelter

Shelter is a basic human need. People have always built shelter. The type of shelter a group built depended on their needs, the climate, and the materials that were available. Some groups moved around a lot. The people in these groups needed to have homes that they could take with them. Other people who lived in cold places had to build their shelter from ice and snow. All of the groups' shelters served the same purpose of protecting the people who lived in them.

1. What is the main idea of this story?
   a. Shelter is a basic human need that comes in many forms.
   b. Building shelter out of ice is easy.
   c. Different groups had different purposes for shelter.

2. Which two words mean the same thing?
   a. ice and mud
   b. shelter and house
   c. basic and need

3. Why would different groups' shelters look different from each other?
   the group's needs, the usual weather of the area, and what they could find to build with

4. Who needed homes they could take with them?
   groups who moved around a lot

5. What purpose does shelter serve?
   protection

6. How might the shelter of someone living in a desert be different from the shelter of someone living in a snowy place?
   Answers will vary.

The Right to Vote

Name _____

Reading about Social Studies

Read the story. Then, answer the questions.

Have you ever voted for class president? Maybe your class has cast votes for the best movie star or type of ice cream. Voting for members of the government is very important. In the United States and Canada, you have to be 18 to vote in one of these elections. Not everyone has been able to vote in the past. In the United States, women were not allowed to vote until 1920. A special law was passed in 1965 to make sure that all adults get to vote. When you vote, you have a say in who serves in the government and what kinds of laws they pass. Some people say that voting is the most important thing that people can do.

1. What is the main idea of this story?
    a. Chocolate ice cream is the best.
    b. Not everyone can vote in the United States.
    c. Voting is an important thing for people to be able to do.

2. Who can vote in the United States and Canada?
    people who are at least 18

3. What happens in an *election*?
    a. People cast votes.
    b. People have to be 18.
    c. People pass laws.

4. When were U.S. women first allowed to vote?
    1920

5. What happened in the United States after a special law was passed in 1965?
    All adults got to vote.

6. Why is voting important?
    Answers will vary.

The U.S. Government

Name _____

Reading about Social Studies

Read the story. Then, answer the questions.

The United States' national government has three branches, or parts. The president leads the country, makes sure that people follow the law, and meets with leaders from other nations. Congress makes laws that apply to people all over the country. Congress has two parts: the Senate and the House of Representatives. The Supreme Court is made up of nine judges who review the laws that Congress passes. Each branch of government has some power over the other two. This means that no one branch can be too powerful. This system of government has worked for over 200 years!

1. What is the main idea of this story?
    a. There are nine judges on the Supreme Court.
    b. The national government has worked for 200 years.
    c. The U.S. government has three parts that have different powers.

2. What does the president of the United States do?
    leads the country, makes sure people follow the law, meets with leaders from other nations

3. What does Congress do?
    makes laws that apply to people all over the country

4. How many judges serve on the Supreme Court?
    nine

5. Why is it important that no branch be too powerful?
    Answers will vary.

Continents

Name _____

Reading about Social Studies

Read the story. Then, answer the questions.

Earth has seven continents: Africa, Antarctica, Asia, Australia, Europe, South America, and North America. All of these continents used to make up one big continent, but over thousands of years the land split. Huge pieces of land drifted apart. The oceans filled in the spaces between the pieces of land. The continents we know today were the result. Each continent looks different and has different plants, animals, and weather than the others. North America does not have tigers, but Asia does. Antarctica does not have a jungle, but South America does. The continents do have similarities too. Some of these similarities seem to be because the seven continents used to be one big piece of land.

1. What is the main idea of this story?
    a. Earth is made of land and water.
    b. Earth has seven continents, which used to be one piece of land.
    c. Earth has many types of animals, plants, and weather.

2. List the seven continents.
    Africa, Antarctica, Asia, Australia, Europe, South America, North America

3. How long did it take for the continents to form?
    thousands of years

4. How are the continents different?
    They have different plants, animals, and weather.

5. Which type of land can you find in South America?
    a jungle

6. Why might continents with an ocean between them have similarities?
    They used to be one big piece of land.

The Liberty Bell

Name _____

Reading about Social Studies

Read the story. Then, answer the questions.

A giant bell called the Liberty Bell stands for freedom in the United States. It measures 30 feet (10 meters) high and 12 feet (3.7 meters) around. The bell was rung in 1776 to call people to hear the Declaration of Independence. This speech told them that the American colonies were breaking away from England to form their own country. The bell has a large crack in it, so it cannot be used anymore. The last time the Liberty Bell was rung was in 1846. Today, the bell stands in Independence Hall in Philadelphia, Pennsylvania. Even though the bell cannot be rung any longer, it still reminds Americans of the people who fought so their country could be free.

1. What is the main idea of this story?
    a. The Liberty Bell stands for freedom.
    b. People fought so they could be free.
    c. The Americans broke away to form their own country.

2. What does the Liberty Bell look like?
    thirty feet high, twelve feet around, has a large crack in it

3. Why was the bell rung in 1776?
    to call people to hear a great speech

4. Where is the Liberty Bell today?
    Philadelphia, Pennsylvania

5. When was the Liberty Bell last rung?
    1846

6. What does the Liberty Bell remind Americans of?
    the people who fought so Americans could be free

Name _____

Reading about Social Studies

Read the story. Then, answer the questions.

Coming to North America

For over 200 years, people from other countries have wanted to come to North America. Many travelers from England and France settled in the northeastern part of North America before the United States was formed. Often, they lived in areas that reminded them of home. Many people from northern Europe ended up in what is now the northern part of the United States and Canada. Others from warmer countries settled farther south. Some people came because they wanted to go to a different type of church than the one their country's government wanted them to. Others came because they had little food or work back home. Travelers to North America were able to start new lives.

1. What is the main idea of this story?
   a. Many settlers traveled south.
   b. People from Europe came to North America.
   c. Europe has people from many different countries.

2. How long have people from other countries been coming to North America?
   over 200 years

3. Who settled in the northeastern part of North America before the United States was formed?
   people from England and France

4. Why did people come to the United States?
   because they wanted to go to a different church or had little food or work

5. What do you think the trip from Europe to North America was like?
   Answers will vary.

88   CD-104304 • © Carson-Dellosa

Name _____

Reading about Social Studies

Read the story. Then, answer the questions.

Going West

As more people moved to the new nation of the United States, people wanted more room. They wanted to raise their families on land that was clean and open. Many decided to move west and traveled in groups of covered wagons. Dusty trail life brought new dangers: snakes, wolves, and robbers. The weather could be very hot or very cold. Many died along the trail. Some people made it all the way to the coast of California. A lucky few found gold in the rivers and mountains there. People who moved west from the eastern United States probably had a strong spirit of adventure.

1. What is the main idea of this story?
   a. More people should move to the western United States.
   b. People in the United States wanting something different moved west.
   c. City life is better than life on a farm.

2. Why did people start moving out of cities in the eastern United States?
   They wanted to raise their families on land that was clean and open.

3. How did many people travel to the west?
   in covered wagons

4. What dangers did trail life bring?
   snakes, wolves, and robbers

5. What did a few people find in California?
   gold in the rivers and mountains

6. What were the people who moved west like?
   They probably had a strong spirit of adventure.

CD-104304 • © Carson-Dellosa   89

Name _____

Reading about Social Studies

Read the story. Then, answer the questions.

Railroads

People may not use railroads much today, but they play an important part in history. For centuries, railroads have helped carry people and goods long distances. In the United States, travel was much harder before a railroad tied together the eastern and western parts of the country. Workers in the eastern United States built a railroad heading west. A different crew in the west started building a railroad heading east. In 1869, the two lines met in the state of Utah. The crews hammered in a special golden nail to tie the two tracks together. After that, people could travel from one coast of the United States to the other! The next time you have to stop at a railroad crossing to let a train go by, think about how important railways have been in history.

1. What is the main idea of this story?
   a. Railroads have an important history in the United States.
   b. No one uses railroads today.
   c. You have to stop to let trains go by.

2. Why was traveling harder before the railroads were built?
   Answers will vary.

3. Where did the two railroads begin?
   one in the east, one in the west

4. Where did the two lines meet?
   Utah

5. Why did the crews use a golden nail?
   Answers will vary.

6. Why do more people still not travel across the United States on a train?
   Answers will vary.

90   CD-104304 • © Carson-Dellosa

Name _____

Reading about Social Studies

Read the story. Then, answer the questions.

Cities and Towns

Do you know the difference between a city and a town? In general, a city is much larger. In a town, you may have only one school that everyone your age goes to. A city may have many schools for people of the same age. They may have sports teams that play each other for a city title. In a town, you may know most of the other people living there. In a city, you may know only the people on your block or in your building. A city may have more money to provide services, but more people are trying to use those services. There are good and bad things about living in either place.

1. What is the main idea of this story?
   a. Cities are better for young people to live in.
   b. There are good and bad things about life in a town or a city.
   c. People in towns never have any money.

2. How are schools different in cities and towns?
   towns—only one school for people of the same age; cities—many schools for people of the same age

3. Who might you know in a town?
   most of the other people living there

4. Who might you know in a city?
   only the people on your block or in your building

5. What are some good and bad things about living in a town?
   Answers will vary.

CD-104304 • © Carson-Dellosa   91

Name _____

Read the story. Then, answer the questions.

Building a Community

A community is a group of people who care about each other. A community might include your neighbors, school, sports teams, or clubs. People will often offer to help others in their communities. You can be useful to each other. You might decide to walk your neighbor's dog or go to the store for your grandmother. Your uncle might watch your cat while your family goes on vacation. A family down the street might ask you if you want to go to the movies. It is important for people to feel like part of a community. Always be kind and thoughtful to the people in your community, even if you do not know their names.

1. What is the main idea of this story?
   a. Your neighbor might ask you to walk his dog.
   b. Everyone likes being in a community.
   c. A community is made up of people who care about each other.

2. What people might a community include?
   your neighbors, school, sports teams, or clubs

3. How might you help someone in your community?
   Answers will vary.

4. How might someone in your community help you?
   Answers will vary.

5. How should you treat people in your community?
   Always be kind and thoughtful.

6. Why do people like to feel they are part of a community?
   Answers will vary.

CD-104304 • © Carson-Dellosa

Name _____

Read the story.

Brad and Amy

Brad and Amy are brother and sister. They both like playing sports. Brad is on the soccer team. "Soccer is better than any other sport," Brad says. Amy likes basketball. She plays at the park down the street. Brad and Amy have a little brother named Steve. Steve would rather read a good book than play sports. He does like to watch his brother and sister play, though. He sits on the sidelines and claps for them. They are both good at their sports!

Decide whether each sentence is a fact (F) or an opinion (O).

F Brad is on the soccer team.

O Soccer is better than any other sport.

F Amy plays basketball at the park.

F Steve is Brad and Amy's little brother.

O Brad and Amy are both good at their sports.

F Steve sits and claps for his brother and sister.

Write a fact from the story.

Answers will vary.

Write an opinion from the story.

Answers will vary.

CD-104304 • © Carson-Dellosa

Name _____

Read the story.

Making Baskets

Today in art class, we made baskets for our mothers. My basket was the best. I put flowers inside of it. I painted the basket purple. Purple is the prettiest color. Then, I drew a picture of my brothers and me. I wrote a note that said "I love you, Mom." She will love it. Next, I will make a basket for my father. His birthday is next week!

Decide whether each sentence is a fact (F) or an opinion (O).

F We made baskets in art class.

O My basket was the best.

O Purple is the prettiest color.

F I drew a picture of my brothers.

O Mom will love the basket.

F My father's birthday is next week.

Write a fact from the story.

Answers will vary.

Write an opinion from the story.

Answers will vary.

CD-104304 • © Carson-Dellosa

Name _____

Read the story.

Dogs and Cats

Dogs come in many different sizes. We have two small dogs and one big one. The big dog is the sweetest. He runs to the door when I come home from school. Then, he licks my hand. He likes to chase balls in the yard. My friend Cara thinks cats are smarter than dogs. Her cat had kittens last summer. Kittens may be cute, but dogs are better pets than cats.

Decide whether each sentence is a fact (F) or an opinion (O).

F We have three dogs.

F My big dog runs to the door.

O He likes to chase balls.

O Cats are smarter than dogs.

F Cara's cat had kittens.

O Dogs are better pets than cats.

Write a fact from the story.

Answers will vary.

Write an opinion from the story.

Answers will vary.

CD-104304 • © Carson-Dellosa

Name _____

Read the story.

Winter Fun

Some people like spring, but not me. Winter is the best season. My family goes to the mountains every year. My stepmom is a good skier. She will ski while we watch. My dad wears snowshoes and goes on long hikes. My brothers and I like to make people out of snow. The nights are too cold to be outside, but we stay warm in our cabin. My stepmom makes us hot cocoa at bedtime, and we tell stories.

Decide whether each sentence is a fact (F) or an opinion (O).

_O_ Winter is the best season.
_F_ My family goes to the mountains.
_O_ My stepmom is a good skier.
_F_ Dad goes on long hikes.
_O_ The nights are too cold.
_F_ My stepmom makes us hot cocoa.

Write a fact from the story.

  Answers will vary.

Write an opinion from the story.

  Answers will vary.

96   CD-104304 • © Carson-Dellosa

Name _____

Read the story.

My Funny Uncle

Uncle Larry is very funny. He tells stories about his life in the circus. He was a famous clown when he was young. He wears silly masks and tells the best jokes. He can make me laugh. It is hard to get my mother to let me stay up late, but when Uncle Larry is in town, it is easy. She lets me stay up and listen to his stories. Someday, I hope I have funny stories of my own because I know I am funny too.

Decide whether each sentence is a fact (F) or an opinion (O).

_O_ Uncle Larry is funny.
_F_ He tells stories about the circus.
_O_ His jokes are the best.
_F_ Uncle Larry can make me laugh.
_O_ It is hard to get my mother to let me stay up late.
_O_ I am funny too.

Write a fact from the story.

  Answers will vary.

Write an opinion from the story.

  Answers will vary.

CD-104304 • © Carson-Dellosa   97

Name _____

Read the story.

Drinking Water

Drinking water is more important than eating. Some people drink several glasses of water every day. Water helps your body work like it should. You want to make sure you drink clean water. You will get sick if you drink water that is dirty. Rainwater is not always clean. Many people drink the water from their kitchen sinks. The water from your kitchen sink has been tested and called safe to drink.

Decide whether each sentence is a fact (F) or an opinion (O).

_O_ Drinking water is more important than eating.
_F_ Some people drink several glasses a day.
_F_ Water helps your body work like it should.
_F_ You will get sick if you drink dirty water.
_F_ Rainwater is not always clean.
_F_ The water from your kitchen sink has been tested.

Write a fact from the story.

  Answers will vary.

Write an opinion from the story.

  Answers will vary.

98   CD-104304 • © Carson-Dellosa

Name _____

Read the story.

I Like Math

Some people think math is hard, but really, it is easy. When my teacher asks someone to go to the board, I raise my hand first. Sometimes, I work extra problems just for fun. My friends ask me for help with their math problems. I explain how to work them differently than the teacher does. My parents are both math teachers. They have shown me all of the tricks I know.

Decide whether each sentence is a fact (F) or an opinion (O).

_O_ Math is easy.
_F_ I raise my hand first.
_O_ Working extra problems is fun.
_F_ My friends ask me for help.
_F_ My parents teach math.
_F_ They show me math tricks.

Write a fact from the story.

  Answers will vary.

Write an opinion from the story.

  Answers will vary.

CD-104304 • © Carson-Dellosa   99

Name _____ Fact or Opinion

Read the story.

Summer Swimming

Swimming is a great way to cool off in the summer. The pool feels wonderful after being in the hot sun. I like to take a picnic to the pool. I daydream and write in my journal. When I get too hot, I jump back in the water. Sometimes, my brother and his friends come along. They like to stay in the pool all day. When I am not looking, they splash me with cold water! You would think it is cold too after being in the sun.

Decide whether each sentence is a fact (F) or an opinion (O).

__O__ Swimming is a great way to cool off.

__O__ The pool feels wonderful.

__F__ I write in my journal.

__F__ I jump back in the water.

__F__ My brother and his friends come along.

__O__ You would think it is cold too.

Write a fact from the story.

Answers will vary.

Write an opinion from the story.

Answers will vary.

100 CD-104304 • © Carson-Dellosa

Name _____ Fact or Opinion

Read the story.

Learning to Cook

My brother is helping me learn to cook. He is an excellent cook. Last night, we made noodles with tomatoes for dinner. We also made a spinach salad. We were going to make a pie, but we were out of ice cream. Pie without ice cream on the side is not very tasty. Our mother loved the meal. We are even better cooks than she is!

Decide whether each sentence is a fact (F) or an opinion (O).

__O__ My brother is an excellent cook.

__F__ We made noodles with tomatoes for dinner.

__F__ We also made a spinach salad.

__F__ We were out of ice cream.

__O__ Pie without ice cream is not very tasty.

__O__ We are better cooks than our mother.

Write a fact from the story.

Answers will vary.

Write an opinion from the story.

Answers will vary.

CD-104304 • © Carson-Dellosa 101

Name _____ Fact or Opinion

Read the story.

Oranges

Oranges are the best fruit. They have a bumpy skin and a sweet taste. You can eat them alone or make orange juice out of them. Orange juice tastes better than lemonade with breakfast. Lemonade is better for a snack. Oranges are hard to peel. Mom cuts my oranges into pieces for my lunch. My friends ask if I will trade for either apples or bananas, but I always say no!

Decide whether each sentence is a fact (F) or an opinion (O).

__F__ Oranges have a bumpy skin.

__F__ You can eat them alone or make juice.

__O__ Lemonade is better for a snack.

__O__ Oranges are hard to peel.

__F__ Mom cuts my oranges into pieces.

__F__ My friends ask if I will trade.

Write a fact from the story.

Answers will vary.

Write an opinion from the story.

Answers will vary.

102 CD-104304 • © Carson-Dellosa

Name _____ Fact or Opinion

Read the story.

Bubbles

My little dog is named Bubbles. We call him that because he tries to eat the soap bubbles in the bath. Bubbles gets a lot of baths because he loves to get dirty. After a rain is the worst. He rolls in the mud. Then, he runs from us as we chase him. It looks like he is laughing at us. Mom gets so mad at him! It is hard to stay mad for long. We just start filling up the tub again.

Decide whether each sentence is a fact (F) or an opinion (O).

__F__ My dog is named Bubbles.

__F__ He tries to eat soap bubbles.

__O__ After a rain is the worst.

__F__ He runs from us as we chase him.

__O__ It is hard to stay mad for long.

__F__ We fill up the tub again.

Write a fact from the story.

Answers will vary.

Write an opinion from the story.

Answers will vary.

CD-104304 • © Carson-Dellosa 103

Congratulations!

receives this award for

Date

Signed

actor	apply	aquarium	artist
banana	bicycle	blaze	blouse
borrow	branch	bubble	business
cactus	carrot	chat	clerk

© CD

coast	crowd	daydream	desk
doorway	drill	dust	govern
either	enjoy	expect	famous
feather	flash	flight	forgive

© CD

friendship	fruit	giant	grand
grape	hammer	harbor	hasty
history	hound	hungry	imagine
island	jingle	journal	knight

© CD

knowledge	ladder	liberty	mask
measure	middle	mountain	nail
narrow	neighbor	only	pleasure
powerful	pretend	proud	prowl

© CD

remove	rainwater	railroad	quart
share	season	result	respect
special	snack	smooth	skill
squeak	spray	spend	speech

© CD

stomach	talent	thick	thirsty
thoughtful	thread	trash	umbrella
useful	vacation	vegetable	wagon
wheat	woodpecker	yank	younger

© CD
© CD
© CD
© CD
© CD
© CD
© CD
© CD
© CD
© CD
© CD
© CD
© CD
© CD
© CD
© CD